DITA 101

Fundamentals of DITA for Authors and Managers

Ann Rockley, Steve Manning and Charles Cooper

Foreword by Scott Abel
Founder of The Content Wrangler

Acknowledgements

This was truly a group effort. I'd like to thank Steve Manning and Charles Cooper for all their assistance in putting this book together.

I would also like to thank Rhonda Truitt and Laurel Simmons who provided edits in a very tight time frame.

We would also like to thank the vendors for providing us with copies of their editors to use to capture examples and create content.

- Adobe FrameMaker
- JustSystems XMetaL
- PTC Arbortext Editor
- Quark Dynamic Publishing Solution for Technical Publications

ISBN 978-0-557-07291-0

For information, contact:

The Rockley Group Inc.,
Email: moreinfo@rockley.com
Website: www.rockley.com

www.dita101.com

Foreword

The pace at which technological innovation occurs is amazing. The last 20 years have been jam-packed with paradigm-shifting technological advances that have altered forever the way we create, manage, and deliver information. The personal computer, the World Wide Web, desktop publishing, touch-screen mobile phones, interactive television, social networks, and wireless connectivity have transformed not only the way consumers interact with content, but these advances have also altered the way professional communicators work.

Nowhere are these changes more evident than in the world of technical communication. Technical writers and editors have been forced – like it or not – to move to a more formal method of creating content, often for a global audience. Gone are the days of the free-for-all approach to creating technical documentation products one-at-a-time using desktop publishing tools. While this technique was the best method possible in the 80s and 90s, today, those who create user manuals, online help systems, and other types of documentation are increasingly expected to take a more formal approach to content creation, utilizing content standards like the Darwin Information Typing Architecture (DITA) - the subject of this book.

The advent of the Extensible Markup Language (XML) and rapid adoption of topic-based content standards like DITA have forced us to separate content from format and end our addiction to desktop publishing. Today, technical communicators must learn to write modular, topic-based, context-independent content using a new breed of authoring tools. It's not an easy change for many. The resources available are often poorly conceived, confusing, jargon-laden collections of information that don't make learning new skills and techniques easy. In fact, they make things much harder than they need be.

That's why DITA 101 by Ann Rockley, Steve Manning and Charles Cooper is such an important work. Simple, easy-to-understand, and loaded with practical examples that resonate with technical communicators, Rockley and team have consolidated years of experience helping folks just like you make the move from unstructured content creation to DITA. This work is the result of their efforts and a valuable contribution to the technical communication literature.

Go ahead, take a peek. It's not as scary as you might think.

Scott Abel, The Content Wrangler

Table of contents

Introduction

More and more companies are either adopting DITA or thinking about adopting it, yet surprisingly, there are very few resources written in plain English for those who want to learn about it. Many of the existing resources are very technical in nature - notably the DITA specification. Often you might find yourself asking "how do I find out more about that?" and the response is, "it is all in the spec."

And there's the problem - the DITA specification is just that - a technical specification describing the standard. It wasn't designed as a teaching tool and it shouldn't be used as one. The spec is something a DITA technologist should read, not the average writer or manager.

The good news is that we've designed DITA 101 *for writers and managers*. We've taken our years of experience helping organizations to move to DITA and distilled it into an easy-to-read and understandable format. And since the move to DITA often goes hand-in-hand with an organization's adoption of content management, we've made sure that our expertise in developing effective content, reuse, and their appropriate strategies are integrated here to give you everything you need to know to understand DITA from a author's or manager's viewpoint.

- *What is DITA* provides a definition of DITA and explains its key features.
- *The value of structure in content* explains how to analyze content for structure and uses recipes to illustrate the concepts of structure and structured writing.
- *Reuse: Today's best practice* presents the benefits of reuse and provides an understanding of all the types of reuse that DITA supports.
- *Topics and maps* takes you through the building blocks of DITA.
- *A day in the life of a DITA author* helps to illustrate how an author would develop a content outline, create topics and write structured content.
- *Planning for DITA* provides insights into how to most effectively plan for DITA and the changes in roles and responsibilities.

- *Metadata* introduces the concepts of metadata, an often overlooked and misunderstood topic, and gives insight into the metadata that DITA supports.
- *DITA and technology* introduces some of the key DITA features that authoring, content management and publishing systems should support.
- *The advanced stuff* contains our insight on such topics as domains, conrefs, selection attributes, relationship tables and specialization.
- *Appendix A and B* provide a quick reference to topic elements and prolog metadata respectively.
- *Appendix C* gives more background on XML if you would like to delve in deeper.

Examples are used throughout to illustrate the concepts.

We hope you find DITA 101 useful.

What is DITA?

There is often a lot of confusion around what DITA really is. Is it a technology? A format? A product? A process? All or any of these things?

Understanding the name

Let's begin with the acronym DITA. DITA stands for **D**arwin **I**nformation **T**yping **A**rchitecture.

Let's look at what this means, but rather than start at the beginning of the acronym, we'll start at the end.

Architecture

A general definition for the word architecture from Wikipedia is:

> *architecture defines the structure and/or behavior of a building or any other kind of system that is to be or has been constructed.*

When building a house, we start with blueprints. The blueprints define how big that house is, where the windows are, where the individual rooms in the house are and how they relate and connect to each other. It's a plan – a roadmap – for building the house. And when it comes to constructing a house, we know there are industry standards that define the sizes of things like a 2 x 4, or sheets of drywall. Without these standards, building a house would be a nightmare. Because we have standard components, we can build houses quickly and efficiently. Yet houses don't all look the same because we take these standard components and use them in interesting and exciting ways. And we can do this with DITA!

In recent years, information architecture for Web sites has become very important. We all know how difficult it is to get around a Web site that is poorly designed. Somtimes a site might be visually attractive, but because the underlying structure is confusing or inconsistent, it's hard to use. Information architects (people who design the structure and navigation of Web sites) use standards and best practices to design a Web site that is easy to navigate and a pleasure to use.

Most organizations have style guides and templates for their materials so that authors create consistently designed and written manuals and Help. But each organization creates guidelines that are unique unto themselves which is fine as long as you don't share your source material with anyone else or need to use their source material. This problem is bad enough *within* organizations; it's multiplied exponentially when companies merge or when rebranding takes place.

When we have guidelines and a common way of structuring our information, it makes that information much easier to create and much easier to share. These are *our* blueprints and 2 x 4s.

IBM (the initial creators of DITA) started with a goal to create commonly structured content for sharing and reuse. So architecture in the context of DITA means:

> *An open content standard that defines a common structure for content that promotes the consistent creation, sharing and reuse of content.*

Information Typing

Let's think about building architecture again. We can easily recognize different types of architecture by some of the features. For example, American Queen Anne architecture has many peaks and often includes a lot of decorative features like brightly painted siding and "gingerbread" (highly ornate trim), while Modernist architecture is comprised of clean lines and smooth uncluttered exteriors. We can identify the type of building we are looking at by its structure and the same holds true for content.

When we analyze content we can also see a number of common kinds (types) of content. For example, on average, technical documentation consists of 60% procedural content.

DITA provides structures for these common types of information:

- Concept – Conceptual (descriptive) information. Used to provide context or understanding.

- Task – Task oriented (procedural) information. Used to define "how to" information.
- Reference – Reference (look-up) oriented information. Used to define specific, often detailed information or to bring together at-a-glance information (e.g., in tables) that is referred to (consulted) on an as required basis.

Just like building a house where we use standard components to build unique structures, we can use standard information types to build unique sets of information. Typing information makes us think more clearly about what kind (or "type") of information we are authoring so that it is consistent and coherent.

The standard set of information types in DITA is small, but you would be amazed at how many different types of information you can author with these three types of information. And when you don't have to think about structure, you can think about the content!

Darwin

Charles Darwin is often described as the "father" of evolution. He was a naturalist who proposed the idea that life has evolved over time from common ancestors.

IBM made the assumption that DITA will evolve over time to support a broader range of information types. In other words, it's not static. If you need another information type such as a troubleshooting topic, then DITA has been designed to make it possible to develop that "specialized" topic and still ensure that it is consistent with the standard information types.

Topics, the building blocks of DITA

DITA was designed to be topic-oriented. This means that you create topics not documents. Topics can easily be mixed and matched with other topics to create different types of documents. And topics can be reused.

Topic-based authoring is not new to most technical communicators. Help is topic-based. Manuals used to be very chapter oriented, but when Help became more common, technical communicators needed to learn how to author smaller chunks of information. Nobody wants to scroll through 10 or more screens of content to read a chapter in a Help file. It's necessary to chunk content into smaller components (topics) so that content is more easily scanned and read online. Each of these smaller chunks of information is known as a topic. And like Help topics, DITA topics are designed to stand on their own with cross-references to other topics.

For more information on topics see "Topics and maps – the basic building blocks of DITA" on page 31.

Maps

In DITA, topics are added into maps to create "documents." Maps are very much like a .book file in FrameMaker where you identify the files you want to include in the book, or a Bill of Materials in manufacturing, but in this case they are topics, not files or products. The book is a compilation of pointers to the files that when published, produces a coherent linear book. A map is a pointer to a set of topics that when published, produces a coherent linear book or Help project.

More and more authors are creating topics for Help rather than manuals and learning to create even smaller chunks of information for social media. You can think of a DITA map like the table of contents in a Help file. When designing a Help project, you can move the topics up or down in the hierarchy or decide that a topic is better presented as a sub-topic of another topic. With a DITA map, you can do exactly the same thing.

For more information on maps in DITA see "Map" on page 41.

Reuse

DITA was specifically designed to support the reuse of content where you "write once, use many." Organizations are increasingly realizing that it makes sense to create content once and reuse it many times rather than rewriting and rewriting and rewriting. DITA makes it extremely easy to include a topic in multiple maps (documents) or even a piece of content like a caution in multiple topics.

Examples of information products that often reuse content are:

- Help, manuals and HTML pages (common content, different outputs)
- Product suite information where there is common functionality across each of the products
- Training and documentation where the training draws on the tasks in the documentation

FrameMaker has always allowed reuse both through books and through text imports for smaller pieces of information, but trying to reuse content in Word has been highly problematic. And trying to reuse content across Help projects has been no easy task either, no matter what the tool! DITA was specifically designed to support reuse.

For more information on reuse see "Reuse: Today's best practice" on page 19.

Content is separate from format

For years and years, it was common for one author to write the manual and another to write the Help. Now we are seeing authors write for mobile devices and social media as well. Sometimes one author does all of the different types of content; sometimes different authors write for different outputs. Aside from being double or triple the work when multiple people write content, multiple authors often make for inconsistent content.

Authors often think that you write differently when authoring for different media, e.g., when authoring for Help or other online materials you have to be more brief or scannable in what you write. But as we said in our book *Managing Enterprise Content: A Unified Content Strategy*

> *In our experience, following guidelines for clear, effective writing makes content usable, regardless of the medium or format in which it appears.*[1]

In the past, moving between one media and another meant manually reformatting the content. This was a lot of work and effort, but creating content separate from format means that different stylesheets can be applied to the content to automatically output to different media.

DITA is specifically designed to separate content from format. It means that you don't think about how the content will look, only how it will read. And you can automatically change the way it looks and how it is delivered with different stylesheets.

Dita defined

To define DITA, let's go back to the original questions:

- Is it a technology?

  DITA is not a technology. As a standard, it is supported by a number of different technologies like authoring tools, content management systems and publishing tools.

- Is it a format?

  DITA is not a format. DITA is implemented in XML.

- Is it a product?

  DITA is not a product, it is an XML standard. The standard is managed by OASIS (Organization for the Advancement of Structured Information Standards). Many people volunteer their time to help in the ongoing growth and definition of DITA.

---

1. Pg. 480.

- Is it a process?

  DITA is not a process, it is an XML standard. However, in order to effectively use DITA, authors will need to change their authoring processes to create structured modular content designed for reuse.

Our definition of DITA is:

> *DITA is an open content standard that defines a common structure for content that promotes the consistent creation, sharing and reuse of content.*

DITA Open Toolkit

A key piece of DITA is the DITA Open Toolkit. The toolkit is essentially a publishing tool. It provides stylesheets for HTML, Help formats and PDF. The DITA Open Toolkit is open source so it is free! If you adhere to the structure of DITA out-of-the box, then you can easily publish your content using the Open Toolkit. You will probably want to modify the stylesheets, but that will require some technical skills.

The value of structure in content

Structure is the hierarchical order in which content occurs in an information product (e.g., user guide, Help, training guide) or topic. Topics have recognizable structures that are repeated each time the information type is created, e.g., a task is always structured in the same way. Structure frees you as the author to think about the content, not always having to think about how content should be organized and written because that's already done for you – as in templates and guidelines that authors have used for years. DITA is more rigorous in making sure that you follow the structure, but it really is not much different than a Word or FrameMaker template.

Structure is everywhere in content. The more consistent the structure, the easier it is for users to read/use and the easier it is for authors to write. When we analyze the structure of content, we use models to help us determine what the best structure for that content is. We build models in spreadsheets – which is a very effective method of displaying and formalizing the hierarchical structure of the content.

We're going to use three recipes to help explain structure and models:

- Anise-Almond Biscotti
- Mediterranean Couscous Salad
- Pecan Pumpkin Cheese Cake

In these examples, the models illustrate the semantic (meaning) structure of the recipes, but do not represent DITA structure. How to map to the DITA structure is illustrated later in this section. Semantic means meaning. Take for example a typical Word file; you have Headings and then a whole lot of Normal. Bullets are tagged Normal, paragraphs of all types are tagged Normal. In the case of our recipe, if you had a Heading then everything else in the recipe was tagged Normal an author would be hard-pressed to figure out what to put in a blank template. However, as soon as we say something is an Ingredient the author knows exactly what to write, and when we say Step then the author knows that an instruction or action is required. Therefore semantic structure makes the structure clear.

Recipe 1

The model that reflects the semantic structure of this recipe is shown in the call-out.

Recipe 1: Anise-Almond Biscotti¶

Ingredients¶

Quantity¤	Ingredient¤	¤
4 tablespoons¤	Butter¤	¤
¾ cup¤	Sugar¤	¤
4¤	Eggs¤	¤
2 ½ cups¤	All purpose flour¤	¤
2 teaspoons.¤	Crushed anise seeds¤	¤
1 ½ teaspoons¤	Baking powder¤	¤
¼ teaspoon¤	Salt¤	¤
1/3 cup¤	Whole blanched almonds¤	¤

Step-by-step¶

1. In a medium-size bowl, beat butter, sugar, and eggs until smooth. Mix in combined flour, anise seeds, baking powder, and salt. Mix in almonds.¶
2. Shape dough on greased cookie sheets into 4 slightly flattened rolls, 1 ½ inches in diameter.¶
3. Bake at 350 degrees until lightly browned, about 20 minutes.¶
4. Let stand on wire rack until cool enough to handle, cut bars into ½ inch slices. Arrange slices, cut sides down on ungreased cookie sheets.¶
5. Bake biscotti at 350 degrees until toasted biscotti are golden on other side and feel
6. Cool on wire racks.¶

¶

Country: Italy¶
Yield: 60 bars (1 serving)¶
Calories: 41¶

Recipe Model for Biscotti	
Element Name	**Element Type**
Recipe	Container
Title	Title
List of Ingredients	Container
Ingredient	Container
Measure	Container
Quantity	Element
Units	Element
Item	Data
Instructions	Container
Step	Element
Country	Element
Yield	Element
Calories	Element

Figure 1: Recipe 1 and associated model.

Recipe 2

This second recipe has a number of differences which include metric and imperial measures (this is a recipe for Canada which uses both measures), a description and has additional nutritional information. A model that reflects the semantic structure for both Recipe 1 and Recipe 2 is shown in the call-out in Figure 2.

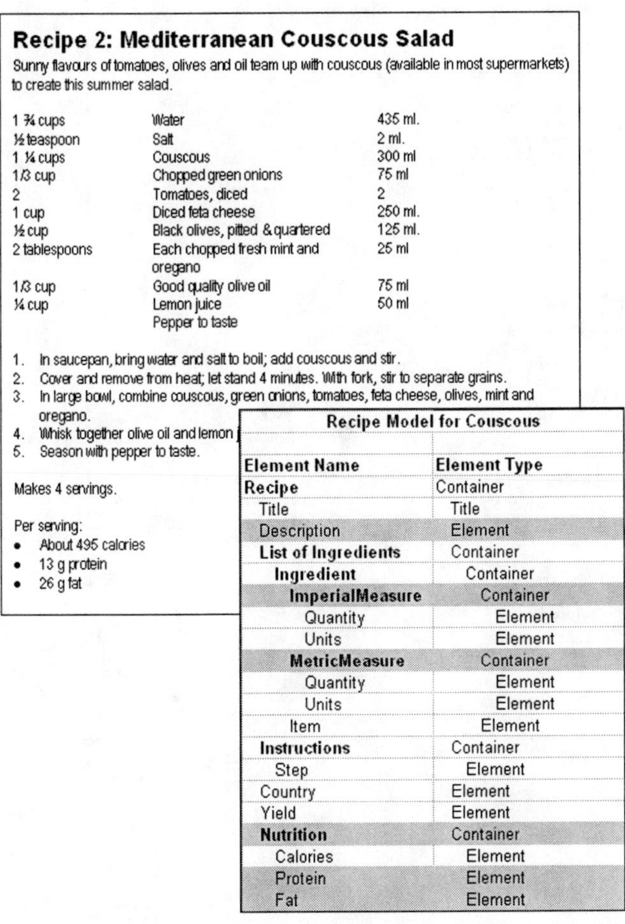

Recipe 2: Mediterranean Couscous Salad

Sunny flavours of tomatoes, olives and oil team up with couscous (available in most supermarkets) to create this summer salad.

1 ¾ cups	Water	435 ml.
½ teaspoon	Salt	2 ml.
1 ¼ cups	Couscous	300 ml
1/3 cup	Chopped green onions	75 ml
2	Tomatoes, diced	2
1 cup	Diced feta cheese	250 ml.
½ cup	Black olives, pitted & quartered	125 ml.
2 tablespoons	Each chopped fresh mint and oregano	25 ml
1/3 cup	Good quality olive oil	75 ml
¼ cup	Lemon juice	50 ml
	Pepper to taste	

1. In saucepan, bring water and salt to boil; add couscous and stir.
2. Cover and remove from heat; let stand 4 minutes. With fork, stir to separate grains.
3. In large bowl, combine couscous, green onions, tomatoes, feta cheese, olives, mint and oregano.
4. Whisk together olive oil and lemon j
5. Season with pepper to taste.

Makes 4 servings.

Per serving:

- About 495 calories
- 13 g protein
- 26 g fat

Recipe Model for Couscous

Element Name	Element Type
Recipe	Container
Title	Title
Description	Element
List of Ingredients	Container
Ingredient	Container
ImperialMeasure	Container
Quantity	Element
Units	Element
MetricMeasure	Container
Quantity	Element
Units	Element
Item	Element
Instructions	Container
Step	Element
Country	Element
Yield	Element
Nutrition	Container
Calories	Element
Protein	Element
Fat	Element

Figure 2: Recipe 2 and associated model that reflects both Recipe 1 and 2.

Recipe 3

Recipe 3 is really a compilation of three recipes and, not surprisingly for a dessert, has no nutritional information. The semantic structure for this recipe is shown in the call-out in Figure 3.

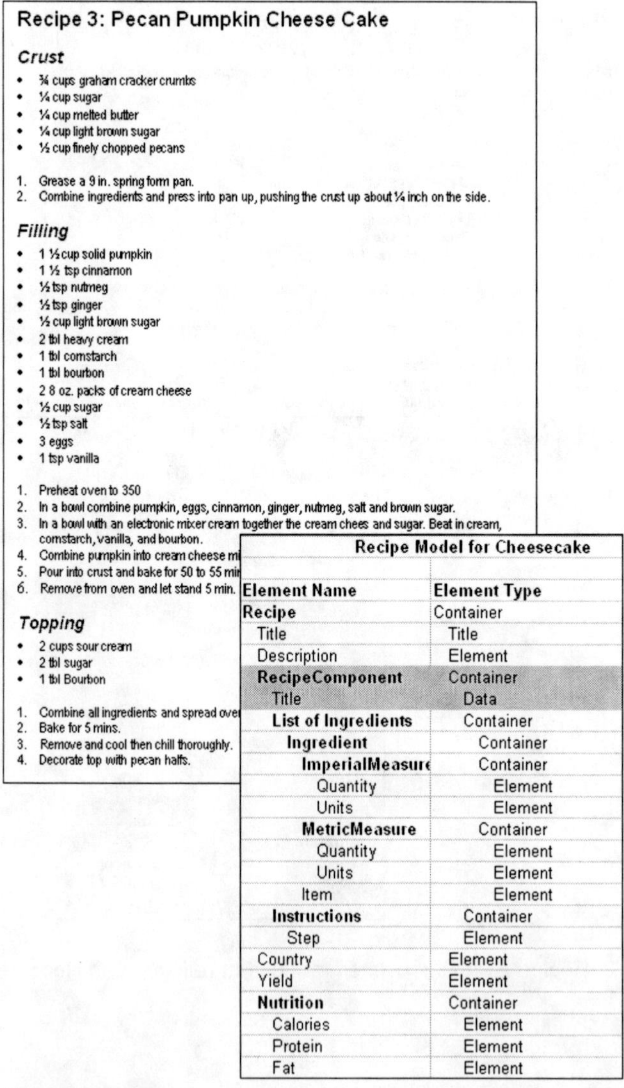

Recipe 3: Pecan Pumpkin Cheese Cake

Crust

- ¾ cups graham cracker crumbs
- ¼ cup sugar
- ¼ cup melted butter
- ¼ cup light brown sugar
- ½ cup finely chopped pecans

1. Grease a 9 in. spring form pan.
2. Combine ingredients and press into pan up, pushing the crust up about ¼ inch on the side.

Filling

- 1 ½ cup solid pumpkin
- 1 ½ tsp cinnamon
- ½ tsp nutmeg
- ½ tsp ginger
- ½ cup light brown sugar
- 2 tbl heavy cream
- 1 tbl cornstarch
- 1 tbl bourbon
- 2 8 oz. packs of cream cheese
- ½ cup sugar
- ½ tsp salt
- 3 eggs
- 1 tsp vanilla

1. Preheat oven to 350
2. In a bowl combine pumpkin, eggs, cinnamon, ginger, nutmeg, salt and brown sugar.
3. In a bowl with an electronic mixer cream together the cream chees and sugar. Beat in cream, cornstarch, vanilla, and bourbon.
4. Combine pumpkin into cream cheese mi
5. Pour into crust and bake for 50 to 55 mi
6. Remove from oven and let stand 5 min.

Topping

- 2 cups sour cream
- 2 tbl sugar
- 1 tbl Bourbon

1. Combine all ingredients and spread ove
2. Bake for 5 mins.
3. Remove and cool then chill thoroughly.
4. Decorate top with pecan halfs.

Recipe Model for Cheesecake

Element Name	Element Type
Recipe	Container
Title	Title
Description	Element
RecipeComponent	Container
Title	Data
List of Ingredients	Container
Ingredient	Container
ImperialMeasur	Container
Quantity	Element
Units	Element
MetricMeasure	Container
Quantity	Element
Units	Element
Item	Element
Instructions	Container
Step	Element
Country	Element
Yield	Element
Nutrition	Container
Calories	Element
Protein	Element
Fat	Element

Figure 3: Recipe 3
and model that reflects all three recipe structures.

The importance of structuring content

By creating and using well-structured content, you create more opportunities for reuse across product lines, audiences and information products. In a structured-authoring environment, when authors follow the same rules or guidelines for each element of content, the potential for reuse is greatly enhanced.

Many problems arise when content is not structured. Not only is unstructured authoring difficult for readers to follow, it's also difficult for authors to create.

Let's take the example of warnings. Without structured authoring guidelines for warnings, some authors may include what happens if users do not comply with the caution, while others may not. And, even if they do include the "result" portion of the warning, they may include different information within it, or use different grammatical structures than other authors. If warnings are to be reusable across information products, they must be structured and written in the same manner, so that their reuse is transparent to both authors and readers.

Benefits of structured content

- Speed – It's faster to create content when there's a pattern to follow. It takes a lot of the guesswork away from trying to figure out structural rules like whether "every task has an introductory paragraph." Having a structure guides the author to create the appropriate content.
- Consistency – When we read or use content, we get used to seeing the same types of information in the same place. When things change (the formatting or structure is different), and there is no obvious reason for the change, our comprehension slows down. Unexpected or unexplainable change reduces the usability of the information. Developing comprehensive, effective structures can eliminate the inconsistencies that drive users mad.
- Predictability – Predictability develops from consistency. When information is consistent in presentation and structure, users get used to the patterns and structures they see. They can find the information faster and understand it easier because of its

predictability. Predictability is also very important for automating publication. It's easier to create stylesheets and automated processing instructions for controlled structures than it is for ad hoc structures.

- Reuse – the creation of structured content ensures that reusable components are truly reusable, that their reuse is transparent and that all content appears unified, whether it is reused or not.

Structured authoring guidelines

Structured authoring is the process of authoring according to standards that dictate how content should be written. When implementing a unified content strategy, it's critical that authors structure and author their content consistently.

The goals of structured authoring are to:

- help authors create consistent content that can be reused transparently
- enhance the usability of content
- make all content appear unified whether it is reused or not

From the viewpoint of modeling, structure is the *hierarchical order* in which the information occurs in the information product. From the viewpoint of authoring, structure is the way *content* within each hierarchical element is written.

Let's use the example of the recipes again. The model for a recipe will specify which elements make up a recipe, which of those elements are mandatory and optional, and the order in which they appear. However, the model does not specify how each of those elements must be written. Even though the model will specify that recipes contain mandatory steps, authors may still write their steps differently. Some authors may include a result as part of their step, some may not. Some authors may describe an ingredient as "tomatoes, diced" while another uses "diced tomatoes." This is where structured authoring comes in. In addition to the architecture (reflected in the models), authors need content development and style guidelines that will help them write content so it is consistent, no matter where it's used and who wrote it.

Structured authoring follows standards. When the structure of the content is defined (for example, the structure of a recipe), whoever writes a recipe must follow that structure. The standard tells authors such things as "a step must always contain the condition under which the step is performed, followed by the action, followed by the result of the action." If all authors follow that standard, ideally, that step can be reused wherever it is needed and its reuse will not be jarring.

Structured authoring guidelines apply to every single element in a model, whether content is planned for reuse or not. Structured authoring guidelines ensure consistency and readability as well as reusability.

Returning to our recipe example, the authoring guidelines for our recipe could be:

Recipe	
Title	Mandatory. Capitalize each word in the title.
Description	Mandatory. Create a short, one or two sentence introduction to the recipe that entices the reader to read on.
List of Ingredients	This is a container for the list of ingredients.
Ingredient	This is a container for the ingredient.
Measure	This is a container for the measure.
Quantity	Optional. For the most part, every ingredient should have a quantity, but in some cases like "pepper to taste" there is no quantity. Enter the quantity for the ingredient.
Units	Mandatory. This is a variable that makes it possible to automatically convert imperial units to metric units.
Item	The name of the ingredient.
Instructions	This is a container for the instructions.
Step	Mandatory. A step must always contain the condition under which the step is performed (e.g., in a medium sized bowl), followed by the action (e.g., mix together the first three ingredients).
Country	Optional. Country of origin.
Yield	Mandatory. Identify how many servings the recipe will make.
Nutrition	This is a container for the nutritional information.
Calories	Mandatory. Identify the number of calories in a single serving.
Protein	Mandatory. Identify the amount of protein in a single serving.
Fat	Mandatory. Identify the amount of fat in a single serving.

Figure 4: Structured authoring sample for recipe model.

Keep in mind that this particular model and associated authoring guidelines do not reflect DITA structure. Authoring guidelines based on a DITA structure can be found in "Writing structured content" on page 48.

When you create authoring guidelines, think about the type of content, how it is being used (as defined in the models), and how it could potentially be reused. Knowing and anticipating how content will be used ensures that guidelines are developed to accommodate all its uses.

An important note though, is that guidelines need to be consistent. Best practices and usability dictate that one guideline should apply to all instances of that structure (e.g., task) even across different information products. These are guidelines, however, and not laws. Occasionally, a task may require authoring something different than what is defined in the guidelines – these execeptions may be driven by specific user needs, or by regulatory requirements. Such cases are few and far between and should not be take as license to ignore the guidelines. However, if you find these changes are required on a regular basis, you should define a different set of guidelines for use. For example, the authoring guidelines for a troubleshooting task guideline would be different from an installation task guideline. Both are valid and acceptable.

When developing authoring guidelines, consider:

- creating standards for each element in an information type (topic).
- always basing standards on usability criteria.
- including an example of a topic written according to the standard so authors have one to follow.
- defining standards that focus on meaning rather than format. Think about what the information should do rather than what the information should look like.
- creating an authoring environment that enables authors to structure their content consistently, by providing them with guidelines and best practice examples of effective structured content.

Reuse: Today's best practice

Content reuse is the practice of using existing components of content to develop new "documents." Text-based materials are the easiest to reuse. It's easier to reuse graphics, charts and media in their entirety than it is to use portions of them, but it is possible to create reusable media. We focus on text-based reuse in this book.

Most organizations already reuse content by copying and pasting content wherever they need it. This works well until the content has to be updated when it's usually very time-consuming to find and change all those places where the content has been used. Not only does this waste time but you run the real danger of missing some instances of content which can result in inconsistencies and inaccuracies.

Then again, a whole lot of organizations write content, rewrite content and then rewrite again! This may be because one of the following is true:

- Multiple people are writing the same or very similar content and do not know that someone else has already written it.
- Everyone feels that their customer and content requirements are different, so the content has to be rewritten.
- Different authors may be assigned to different media (e.g., one author is responsible for Help, while another is responsible for print and yet another for training materials).
- Some authors feel it's just too hard to find what is already written, and therefore, it's much faster to write the content from scratch.

Why reuse content?

When we write content for technical documents, particularly when we have product suites, product solutions and common functionality, there are many good reasons for reusing content.

Reusing content can provide a dramatic improvement in the way content is created in an organization. Improvements include increased quality and consistency, reduced time and costs for development and maintenance and reduced costs of translation.

Reduced development, review and maintenance

Development costs are reduced because the amount of content a author has to create is reduced. Authors do not have to research and write it again, they simply reuse it.

In addition to taking less time to create the content, less time is required to review the content. When approved content is reused, it's not necessary to review it again. This frees up reviewers to do their "real job."

When content is reused, everywhere that content is reused is automatically updated.

ROI: Is based on the percentage of reuse. Typically this is a minimum of 25%, but could be as high as 80%, depending upon how the content is reused (e.g., across types of information such as Help and print, the percentage of reuse is often very high and is also high across variations of a product).

Translation

You can significantly reduce the cost of translation through reuse. Translation memory systems (TMS) use pattern matching to match content that has already been translated so the content does not have to be translated again. Each time content is sent for translation, it's run through the translation memory tool to identify content strings (text) that have been already translated and the existing translation is reused. As you plan for reuse, you ensure that more content is reused, and therefore translation costs are reduced even further. In addition, if content has already been translated, only new or changed content needs to be sent out for translation which reduces costs even more.

Translated content can also be rapidly reconfigured and brand new information products can even be delivered from existing elements that have already been translated, without ever having to send that content to translation and pay additional costs.

The less easily measured benefits of consistent structure, consistent terminology and standardized writing guidelines that reuse requires also help to reduce the cost of translation.

Often, a large cost in translation is in reformatting content. Frequently, content must be converted from the original source format (e.g., Help, FrameMaker, HTML) to RTF (rich text format) before it can be translated. When it's converted, it loses much of its formatting. When content is in XML (e.g., DITA), it's easy to automatically reformat content, regardless of language.

ROI: One of the biggest areas of ROI for DITA and reuse is with translation. If four or more languages are translated, typically all costs can be recouped in less than 18 months (including the cost of purchasing a content management system). Some specific areas of translation ROI include:

- The cost of translation is reduced by the percentage of reuse (typically a minimum of 25%).
- The cost of reviewing the translated content is also reduced by the percentage of reuse.
- Desktop publishing/post translation formatting is typically reduced by 30-50%.

Increased consistency

When there is no reuse, the chances of inconsistencies in content increases, either because the content has been rewritten by many people, or because it has been copied and pasted and some of the occurrences of the content have not been updated properly. Often, when content is copied and pasted, the versions of the content begin to diverge over time.

When samples of materials are examined, examples where content is similar, but not exactly the same are found. On average, five to six variations of content are found. The worst we have seen is 56! Yet, nine times out of ten, when we and our client really look at the information, we realize that the content could be identical.

When content is written once and reused many times, it ensures that the content is consistent wherever it is used. This consistency leads to higher quality content.

ROI: ROI is based on cost avoidance.

Rapid reconfiguration

Reusable content is modular content (small self-contained topics that can be used in combination with other topics). In today's rapidly changing world, products and customer requirements are constantly changing. Modular reusable content makes it easy for organizations to rapidly reconfigure their content to meet changing needs. You can easily change the order of modules, include new modules, exclude existing modules and use modules to build entirely new information products to meet new needs.

ROI: The ROI for rapid configuration is the opportunity cost.

Real world examples of the benefits of reusing content

High Technology

A high tech firm found an error and documented how to avoid the problem. The change was documented in a technical bulletin, but it never made it back to the site alerts or regular documentation. All of a sudden, customer systems started failing, resulting in millions of dollars of lost revenue and very unhappy customers! The problem was most customers had not read the technical bulletin and because the information did not show up anywhere else, they were not aware of it.

Medical Devices

A medical devices firm was hit with a $10,000,000 lawsuit. Content in the Physician's Guide was different from content in the Patient's Guide which was different from what was on the Web site. A doctor provided guidance to a patient who went back to the documentation to remember what to do. The documentation was wrong and the patient ended up being hospitalized. The medical devices firm lost the lawsuit.

Processes of reuse

There are multiple methods of reusing content.

Opportunistic reuse

Opportunistic reuse occurs when the author makes a conscious decision to find an element, retrieve it and reuse it. Opportunistic reuse is the most common form of reuse. However, opportunistic reuse relies on the motivation of the author to know that reusable content exists and to go and find it.

Any content can be used in an opportunistic reuse situation. In some ways, opportunistic reuse is a replacement for "copy and paste." However, opportunistic reuse is not copy and paste because it's actually a "pointer" to the source content.

Systematic reuse

Systematic reuse is planned reuse. If you have a component content management system, it can automate this type of reuse. Specific content is identified as reusable in a particular place and is automatically inserted. This can be done at authoring (e.g., as a specific template is used and content identified) or at delivery (e.g., personalization).

Systematic reuse can significantly increase the percentage of reuse because reuse can be planned and ensured. However, systematic reuse requires a greater level of information architecture to identify and implement the opportunities for reuse.

Types of reuse

DITA was specifically designed for reuse. Topics, sections, paragraphs, sentences, or even words can be reused. The types of reuse will be described here and how you accomplish reuse with DITA will be described in more detail later in the book.

DITA supports a number of different types of reuse including:

Topic-based reuse

Topic-based reuse is the process in which authors create content as individual topics. Topic-based reuse is at the heart of DITA. "A topic is a discrete piece of content that is about a specific subject, has an identifiable purpose, and can stand alone."[1] Authors assemble topics to create information products and topics are assembled together into information products using DITA maps (see "Map" on page 41). For example, the third recipe we showed you for pumpkin cheesecake could be assembled as a map of three topics, each of which is a recipe.

Figure 1: Topic-based reuse within a recipe

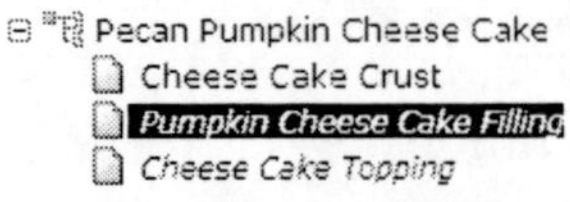

Topic-based writing can sometimes be the hardest thing authors need to learn to do when moving to DITA. Guidelines for how to create topic-based content can be found in "What is a topic " on page 46.

Fragment-based reuse

Pieces of a topic, like a paragraph or a section can also be reused. This is referred to as fragment-based reuse because a fragment (piece) of a topic is used. A fragment may include a title like a topic does, but it also may be a paragraph or even a sentence. In the past, to reuse a small piece of information like a paragraph, the content had to be chunked out and saved as an individual piece/file of information. DITA makes it possible to point to any structure in a topic

---

1. http://en.wikipedia.org/wiki/Topic-based_authoring

(e.g., p [paragraph], stepxmp [step example]) and identify that we want to reuse that information. This makes small fragments of information much more manageable.

Fragment-based reuse can either be opportunistic (known content exists so the author takes the opportunity to find it or reuse it) or systematic (planned reuse). It's not possible to have writing best practices for opportunistic reuse, but it is for systematic reuse. While any element in any topic can be pointed to and identified for reuse, it makes a lot of sense to group together content planned for reuse (systematic reuse). For example, if a author wants to reuse a warning, the author could point to it in the topic that includes it, but the next author who wants to reuse that warning would have a very difficult time knowing where that warning is located to reuse it. It makes more sense to group together commonly reused content fragments into a single topic for ease of search and retrieval. Or in the case of the recipes, you could group together the descriptions of different ingredients such as couscous which is a type of pasta.

Fragment-based reuse is supported in DITA with conrefs (see "Conrefs" on page 82). For example, we could create a Pasta topic that provides more detail on different types of pasta and reuse the fragment on couscous into the recipe.

·<enter·topic·title·here>Pasta¶

·¶
Couscous·is·a·very·tiny·pasta·that·originated·in·North·Africa.¶
¶
Penne·are·tube-shaped·pasta·with·angled·ends·cut·to·resemble·a·quill·or·pen·point.·Penne·pasta·means·"pen"·in·Italian.·¶
¶
Farfalle·are·rectangular·or·oval·pieces·of·pasta·that·are·pinched·in·the·middle.·They·look·like·bow·ties.·Farfalle,·means·"butterfly"·in·Italian.·¶
¶

<enter task title here>Mediterranean Couscous Salad

Sunny flavors of tomatoes, olives and oil team up with couscous (available in most supermarkets) to create this summer salad.

Pre-requisites

1 ¾ cups	Water	435 ml.
½ teaspoon	Salt	2 ml.
1 ¼ cups	Couscous	300 ml
1/3 cup	Chopped green onions	75 ml
2	Tomatoes, diced	2
1 cup	Diced feta cheese	250 ml.
½ cup	Black olives, pitted & quartered	125 ml.
2 tablespoons	Each chopped fresh mint and oregano	25 ml
1/3 cup	Good quality olive oil	75 ml
¼ cup	Lemon juice	50 ml
	Pepper to taste	

Context Information

Couscous is a very tiny pasta that originated in North Africa.

1. In a saucepan, bring water and salt to boil; add couscous and stir.
2. Cover and remove from heat; let stand 4 minutes. With fork, stir to separate grains.
3. In large bowl, combine couscous, green onions, tomatoes, feta cheese, olives, mint and oregano.
4. Whisk together olive oil and lemon juice; pour over salad and toss to combine.

Figure 2: Couscous fragment reused in the Mediterranean Couscous Salad recipe. Note that the authors structural cues like "task title" and "context" have been deliberately left in the image for understanding.

Filtered reuse

In filtered reuse, authors provide variants for a specific chunk of information in a single component. The variations are identified by conditional tags or attributes. When the topic is "published," the different variations are published as required.

Filtered reuse is very valuable in multichannel publishing, audience variants, product variants, region variants and so on. It's an intuitive way for authors to keep all variations together for ease of writing and review.

Also, all the variants must be written and structured in such a way that they are consistent with other content they will be used with. For example, if a variant element includes content for training, a user guide and for online Help, the content that is published to Help must be structured in such a way that it is consistent with the other content written for the Help file. The same goes for training and for the user guide.

We sometimes refer to the creation of filtered reuse as the "building block" approach. That's because there's a core set of content that's applicable in all uses and variant content that *builds* on the core content that is only applicable in certain situations. To create content for filtered reuse:

- Identify the core content (the content that is applicable for all uses).
- Identify what has to be added, what has to differ to meet other needs.
- Make sure that when the content is filtered (e.g., the irrelevant content is filtered out), the content still flows.
- Tag the elements, indicating where they belong.

Use of the building block approach allows authors to create all the content for a reusable element at the same time; in this way, all reusable content for an element resides together and can be reused in its entirety.

Filtered reuse is often thought of as conditional reuse, (e.g., like conditionals in FrameMaker) and is accomplished using Selection Attributes in DITA (see “Selection attributes (conditional content)” on page 84). Attributes is another name for metadata. (Refer to “Metadata” on page 61 for more information on metadata.) In FrameMaker you would create a condition tag, in DITA you create a tag (attribute) for selecting the content to hide or show when content is published.

For example, we could decide to filter the description for couscous and only display it for novice cooks. In this case, we have created an attribute (tag) called Audience that has a value of Novice that lets us show the description for couscous in the Novice version of the recipes, but hide the couscous description for more experienced cooks.

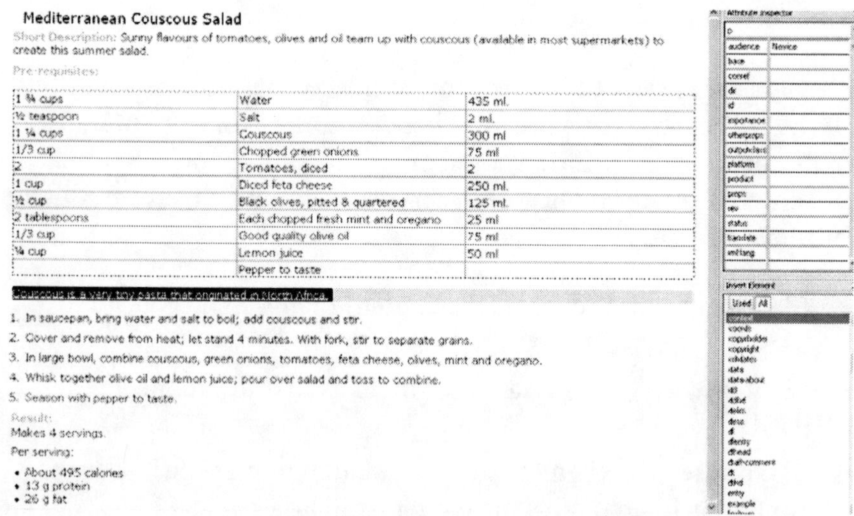

Figure 3: Illustrates the Audience value of Novice applied to the couscous description.

Variable reuse

Variable reuse occurs when a variable is set up that can have a different value in different situations. For example, the name of a product might be one thing in North America and another in the European Union. Variable reuse is very useful for small pieces of information.

Variable reuse becomes valuable when there are only slight variations in content (such as product names in different regions), but otherwise the rest of the content is identical.

When creating the values for variables, remember that the value has to transparently fit into the content so that the content flows like a regular sentence that does not include a variable.

Looking closely at the recipes, it's obvious they are written by different people, particularly when looking at the measurements. There is tablespoon, tbl and tbsps. These should be consistent. You could use a variable to control the terminology used for measures. Variables are also supported with conrefs. Refer to "Conrefs" on page 82 to see how variables can be accomplished using DITA.

Topics and maps – the basic building blocks of DITA

DITA provides the first formal approach to offering component-based markup for content and publishing. By component-based, we mean that outputs are built by combining components of content and processing (publishing) them using stylesheets to produce output (print, Help, Web). In DITA, the major components – the basic building blocks of any output – are "topics." The mechanism for putting the topics together is the "DITA map."

Once, when we presented these concepts at a workshop, an attendee responded with "then this is something like Web pages (as topics) and site map (as DITA map)." Yes... and no. In HTML, the markup or tags define how the content appears and can suggest structure. In DITA, the tagging defines the content structure. A site map represents the "output" - the physical pages that are in place on a site. A DITA map represents "input" to the process. A DITA map is not delivered as output, but is used to manage the collection and conversion of content from topics to output, whether HTML, PDF, etc. The DITA map could be used to create a site map, but it does not have to match the site map.

Generic topic

In DITA, all types of topics evolved from the basic generic topic. We will refer to Generic topic as "topic." It contains the basic structures that are required of any type of topic. It is defined with a relatively simple structure, including:

- title
- short description (or abstract)
- prolog (for metadata)
- topic body
- related links

These are not all of the elements, but we regard these as the key elements. Let's look at each of these elements in greater detail.

Title

The title element is pretty much self explanatory. Some of the things to consider in a title element are:

- The title is not mandatory because topics can exist without titles.
- Alternate titles can be specified for things like search results and TOCs; this is really useful for things like long titles that will not fit in XHTML widgets or other TOC mechanisms.

Short description/abstract

The short description element (shortdesc) is an interesting type of content. Its definition from the language specification is as follows:

"The short description (<shortdesc>) element occurs between the topic title and the topic body, as the initial paragraph-like content of a topic, or it can be embedded in an abstract element. The short description, which represents the purpose or theme of the topic, is also intended to be used as a link preview and for searching."

This last sentence is extremely important, as it highlights one of the key characteristics of DITA, namely the relationship between the DITA elements and the default behaviors of the DITA toolkit.

As shortdesc is "intended to be used as a link preview and for searching," it has been defined with a very simple structure. No paragraphs, just text and inline elements. This makes sense because when you think about it, users don't want multiple paragraphs showing up in link descriptions or search results. The toolkit was designed accordingly to include the shortdesc as link previews for parent topics.

This then raises the following question: does it make sense to have the first paragraph of the topic and link and search previews the same? It might, but it might also be better to have them slightly different.

For example, consider the Couscous recipe, which has the following description:

> *"Sunny flavours of tomatoes, olives and oil team up with couscous (available in most supermarkets) to create this summer salad."*

This example works as the initial paragraph of the recipe and in search results and link previews.

The alternative to shortdesc is abstract. Its description from the language specification is as follows:

> *"The abstract element occurs between the topic title and the topic body, as the initial content of a topic. It can contain paragraph-level content as well as one or more shortdesc elements which can be used for providing link previews or summaries."*

Abstract can be used to create a more thorough introduction (more than one paragraph) and shortdesc can be used to provide the previews to help users navigate the output and find topic.

Note that the shortdesc for an element in a map or bookmap can also be defined as part of the topicmeta structure of a topicref (or other map or bookmap elements). A default shortdesc can be defined in the topic and overridden in the map if necessary. Abstract in a map cannot be overridden, but still can be defined as a shortdesc in a map to override a shortdesc in a topic.

Prolog (for metadata)

The prolog element contains the topic metadata of all sorts. It contains the metadata that we normally use for things like project tracking, including

- author
- source
- publisher
- copyright
- critical dates
- permissions

These metadata elements help to manage the project, as well as provide additional information for finding and manipulating topics.

The prolog element also contains the metadata element, in which the more contextual information about the topic is stored. Sub-elements include:

- audience
- category
- keywords
- prodinfo
- othermeta

Topic body

The topic body is the element that contains the bulk of the real information in the topic. In generic topic, topicbody is defined to contain the most commonly used HTML tags for structure (p, ul, ol, table, dl), along with the addition of a section element, which allows you to the break up a long topic into sections. (The use of HTML elements where appropriate is common throughout the topic structures.) Currently, sections cannot be nested (e.g., section (e.g., subsection) within a section), although there is discussion about nested sections for the future.

It's in the body element (and we're using body generically here), that the specialized types of concept, task and reference diverge from topic. Each has a "body" element that is specific to the topic type. Concept has conbody, task has taskbody and reference has refbody.

Related links

The related-links element is a special section at the end of the topic for pointers to related topics and information. Although they may seem very self-explanatory, you have to be careful about hard coding cross-references in the related links section. You must be sure that all the target topics will always be there.

Consider using reltables for related links when topics are expected to be reused. Feel free to include cross-references to things like external Web sites. For example, a pointer to Microsoft.com is probably safe.

A sample topic

To illustrate the markup that might be used for a topic, here are two recipes created as generic topics.

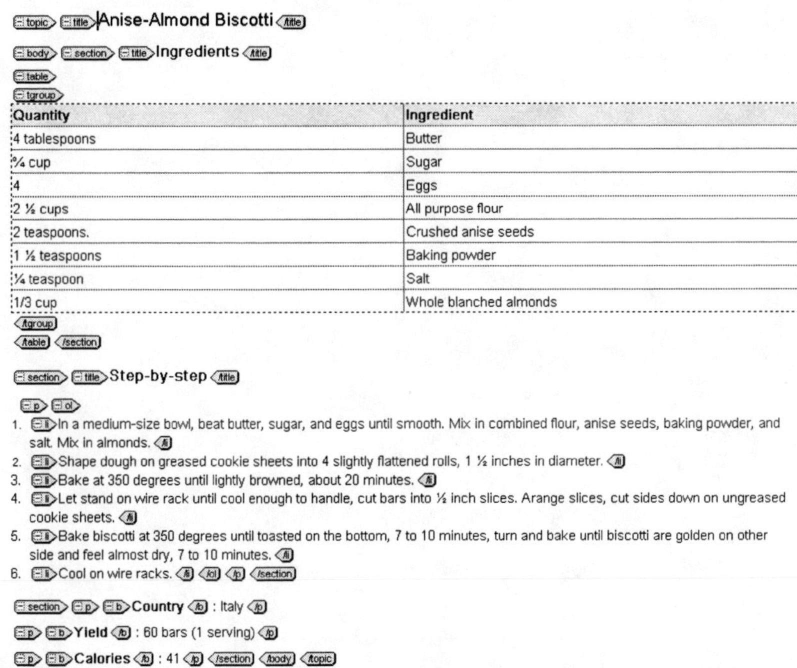

Anise-Almond Biscotti

Ingredients

Quantity	Ingredient
4 tablespoons	Butter
¾ cup	Sugar
4	Eggs
2 ½ cups	All purpose flour
2 teaspoons.	Crushed anise seeds
1 ½ teaspoons	Baking powder
¼ teaspoon	Salt
1/3 cup	Whole blanched almonds

Step-by-step

1. In a medium-size bowl, beat butter, sugar, and eggs until smooth. Mix in combined flour, anise seeds, baking powder, and salt. Mix in almonds.
2. Shape dough on greased cookie sheets into 4 slightly flattened rolls, 1 ½ inches in diameter.
3. Bake at 350 degrees until lightly browned, about 20 minutes.
4. Let stand on wire rack until cool enough to handle, cut bars into ½ inch slices. Arange slices, cut sides down on ungreased cookie sheets.
5. Bake biscotti at 350 degrees until toasted on the bottom, 7 to 10 minutes, turn and bake until biscotti are golden on other side and feel almost dry, 7 to 10 minutes.
6. Cool on wire racks.

Country : Italy

Yield : 60 bars (1 serving)

Calories : 41

Figure 1: Biscotti recipe captured in a generic topic

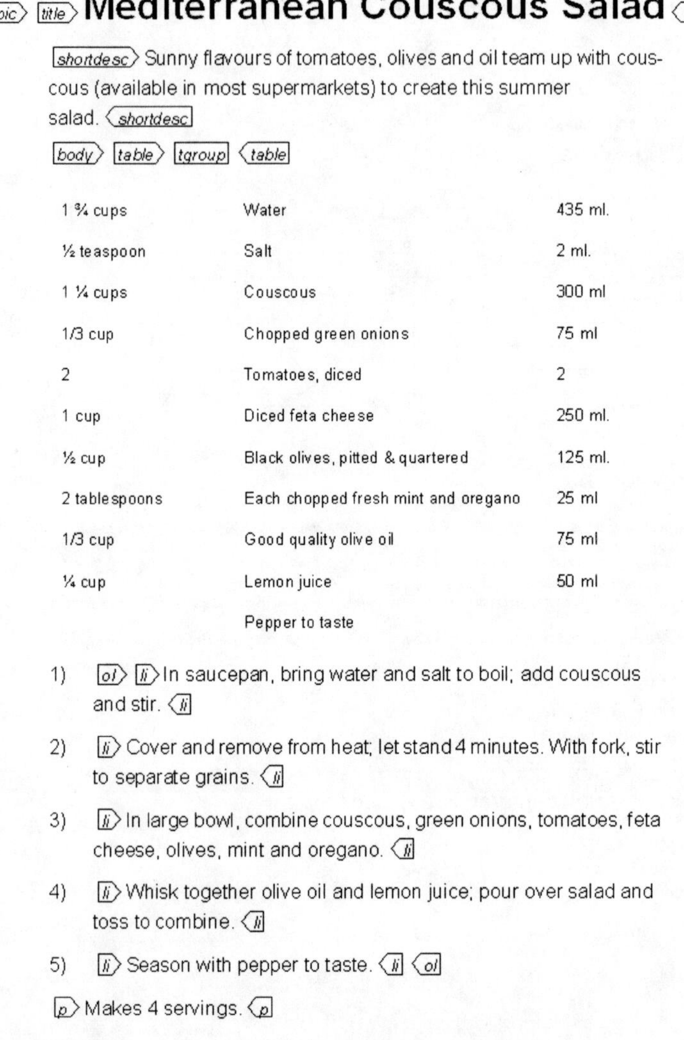

Mediterranean Couscous Salad

Sunny flavours of tomatoes, olives and oil team up with couscous (available in most supermarkets) to create this summer salad.

1 ¾ cups	Water	435 ml.
½ teaspoon	Salt	2 ml.
1 ¼ cups	Couscous	300 ml
1/3 cup	Chopped green onions	75 ml
2	Tomatoes, diced	2
1 cup	Diced feta cheese	250 ml.
½ cup	Black olives, pitted & quartered	125 ml.
2 tablespoons	Each chopped fresh mint and oregano	25 ml
1/3 cup	Good quality olive oil	75 ml
¼ cup	Lemon juice	50 ml
	Pepper to taste	

1) In saucepan, bring water and salt to boil; add couscous and stir.
2) Cover and remove from heat; let stand 4 minutes. With fork, stir to separate grains.
3) In large bowl, combine couscous, green onions, tomatoes, feta cheese, olives, mint and oregano.
4) Whisk together olive oil and lemon juice; pour over salad and toss to combine.
5) Season with pepper to taste.

Makes 4 servings.

Figure 2: Couscous recipe captured in a generic topic

Notice that the markup used is very generic. A section is used to provide headings for Ingredients and Steps. Plain tables are used for ingredients and an ordered list (with the familiar HTML ordered list <ol> tag) for instructions. Simple bold tags are used for origin and nutrition information.

This could be quite workable for publishing the recipes. But with very generic tagging, there are risks as well. Structurally, DITA does not really provide semantic tagging (tagging that has meaning, like our model of the recipe) which could make the process of creating the recipes more difficult. This DITA looks more like HTML than useful DITA. By using tags in a semantic manner, and by choosing an appropriate DITA information type (task, rather than generic in this case), we can actually begin to harness the advantages of DITA. See "Task example" on page 38.

Concept

The concept topic type is intended to capture content that tells you "what something is." When you are describing the core knowledge that someone needs to understand how a product works or operates or how pieces of product relate, use the concept topic type.

The concept topic type is identical in structure to generic topic with one exception: instead of the body element, concept has a conbody. Otherwise, it still follows the title, shortdesc, ... structure. The conbody also contains the same structure as body.

With such seemingly inconsequential differences, one might ask why use concept at all? Why not just use topic for concept? The answer is that using concept as the type of topic instantly identifies the type of content being captured. It indicates what someone should expect if they are reviewing the topic in a repository, it helps remind authors of the type of information they are trying to write and it makes it easier to find the content when searching for topics to reuse or point to as a related link.

Task

The task topic type is used to capture "how to" information. Like concept, it defines type specific structures in the body element, in this case called taskbody. The taskbody structure is semantically very specific, with the following sub-structure:

- pre-requisite
- context

- steps
- result
- example
- post-requisite

All of these elements are optional. Context is intended to give "background information on the task." Some have argued that it would be better placed before the pre-requisite, but then again, things can be moved around with stylesheets as you see fit.

The steps element contains one or more step elements. The sub-structure of step is again quite semantic and provides the structure for each and every command in the procedure:

- command
- information
- substeps
- tutorial information
- step example
- choices
- stepresult

The command describes the action that the user must perform and is the only required element in the structure.

Task example

Since a recipe is basically a procedure for creating a certain dish, it might make sense to capture them as tasks rather than generic topics. Therefore the Biscotti recipe is captured using the task structures (Figure 3) to illustrate the step-by-step structures of DITA.

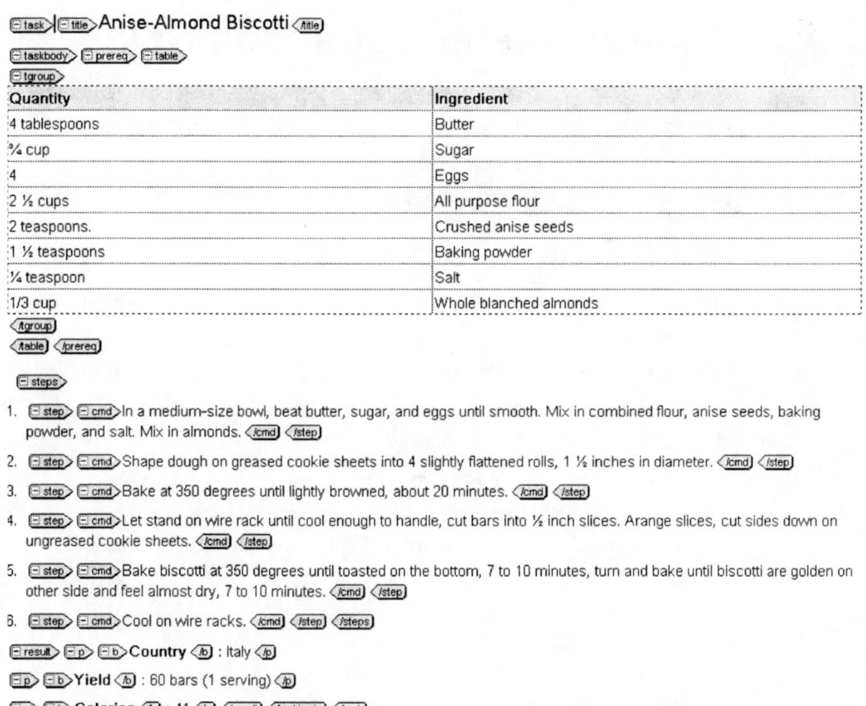

Anise-Almond Biscotti

Quantity	Ingredient
4 tablespoons	Butter
¾ cup	Sugar
4	Eggs
2 ½ cups	All purpose flour
2 teaspoons.	Crushed anise seeds
1 ½ teaspoons	Baking powder
¼ teaspoon	Salt
1/3 cup	Whole blanched almonds

1. In a medium-size bowl, beat butter, sugar, and eggs until smooth. Mix in combined flour, anise seeds, baking powder, and salt. Mix in almonds.
2. Shape dough on greased cookie sheets into 4 slightly flattened rolls, 1 ½ inches in diameter.
3. Bake at 350 degrees until lightly browned, about 20 minutes.
4. Let stand on wire rack until cool enough to handle, cut bars into ½ inch slices. Arange slices, cut sides down on ungreased cookie sheets.
5. Bake biscotti at 350 degrees until toasted on the bottom, 7 to 10 minutes, turn and bake until biscotti are golden on other side and feel almost dry, 7 to 10 minutes.
6. Cool on wire racks.

Country : Italy

Yield : 60 bars (1 serving)

Calories : 41

Figure 3: Biscotti captured using task

In the recipe, the origin and nutritional information is captured in the results element. You could argue that these are not really results, so it might be a bad choice. The information could have been put in a post-requisite element following the steps. However, that type of information is not really the sort of thing that would be considered post-requisite. The information could also be captured in context elements, where it makes more sense contextually. It might be a little confusing for people creating the recipes to see this sort of relationship between ingredients and steps, but stylesheets could be modified to output the information following the steps for the end users. It's a real benefit of stylesheets that content can be moved around. Otherwise this fits pretty well, even though just a very small subset of the tagging in the steps structure is used.

For comparison, we also captured the Couscous recipe in the task structure (Figure 4).

<task> <title> Mediterranean Couscous Salad </title>

<shortdesc> Sunny flavours of tomatoes, olives and oil team up with couscous (available in most supermarkets) to create this summer salad. </shortdesc>

<taskbody> <prereq> PREREQUISITE

<table> <tgroup> </table> </prereq>

1 ¾ cups	Water	435 ml.
½ teaspoon	Salt	2 ml.
1 ¼ cups	Couscous	300 ml
1/3 cup	Chopped green onions	75 ml
2	Tomatoes, diced	2
1 cup	Diced feta cheese	250 ml.
½ cup	Black olives, pitted & quartered	125 ml.
2 tablespoons	Each chopped fresh mint and oregano	25 ml
1/3 cup	Good quality olive oil	75 ml
¼ cup	Lemon juice	50 ml
	Pepper to taste	

TASK

1. <steps> <step> <cmd> In saucepan, bring water and salt to boil; add couscous and stir. </cmd> </step>
2. <step> <cmd> Cover and remove from heat; let stand 4 minutes. With fork, stir to separate grains. </cmd> </step>
3. <step> <cmd> In large bowl, combine couscous, green onions, tomatoes, feta cheese, olives, mint and oregano. </cmd> </step>
4. <step> <cmd> Whisk together olive oil and lemon juice; pour over salad and toss to combine. </cmd> </step>
5. <step> <cmd> Season with pepper to taste. </cmd> </step> </steps>

Figure 4: Couscous captured using task

Compare the tagging shown in Figure 4 with the tagging shown in Figure 2. Note how the entire recipe has been defined as "task," and how the numbered steps are identified as "step" rather than just as items in a list. Step is much more semantic than list item <li>.

Reference

The reference type is intended for documenting the sort of lookup information found in tables, or for documenting the "structural" components of a product. For example, in the software world, reference is used for documenting things like screens, functions and interface details.

Following the same pattern as task and concept, reference has a unique body element called refbody, which defines the elements that might be needed for documenting an interface or presenting tabular data.

Map

The map structure is one of the key characteristics that gives DITA its strong reuse capability.

When a map is created, a series of topic references are added that point to the topics to include in the output when the map is processed. Hierarchical relationships can be created by creating topic references inside of other topic references. The outer topic becomes the parent of the topics it contains. In this way, the map represents the output to produce.

What makes the map/topic relationship so powerful is that topics are never embedded in the map. The map points to the topic that should be included in the output. To illustrate, consider the Biscotti recipe. If you were creating a book of favorite Italian recipes, you could include the recipe in a Dessert section, as in Figure 5.

Figure 5: Map 1- Italian Favorites cookbook

If you were then asked to create a new book that featured only dessert recipes, this time focusing on regional favorites, you might include the Biscotti recipe in this new structure, as shown in Figure 6.

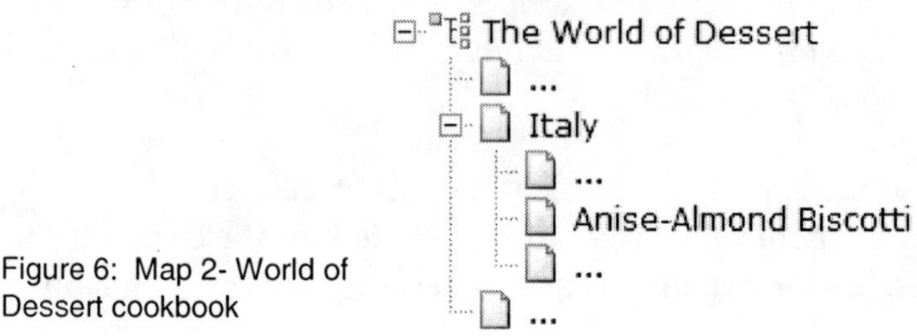

Figure 6: Map 2- World of Dessert cookbook

The key here is that only one Biscotti topic was created and can be used with minimal effort in as many different books as desired. The topic can be moved to different levels in hierarchy and the topic never has to be touched.

There are lots of other things that can be done in a map including applying metadata to the topicrefs (pointers to the topics in the map) to override (or supplement) metadata in the topic. This is effective for reuse. Certain values for metadata for a topic in one map can be applied, while applying different values for the same topic in a different map.

Finally, other ditamaps can be pointed to using topicrefs (in this case a pointer to a map).

Bookmap

DITA has been a tough sell among those creating books as output, rather than Help files or other types of output. For the book-focused authors, there were no structures in DITA that could accommodate the needs of front matter, back matter, part, or chapter structure. With version 1.1, a new DITA bookmap structure specialized from the generic map, was added to support book output.

At its core, bookmap is very similar to base ditamaps. Topics are aggregated in a bookmap by pointing to them from topicrefs. However, bookmap also supports book structures that were missing, including:

- book metadata
- frontmatter
- chapter
- part
- appendix
- back matter

The book metadata is significant, as it includes a lot of elements that are absolutely necessary to the book publishing industry. The front matter element includes the structures that you need for things like colophon pages, copyright notices, book abstracts and prefaces.

Chapter, part and appendix provide elements with which to group topics into the standard structures of books. There is the option to add metadata and any level of division to control processing of child topics.

The front matter and back matter elements allow the capture of the types of information that are appropriate to the front or back of the book, including booklists, notices, dedication, colophon, book abstract, draft information, preface and amendments.

For example, we've implemented our "Italian Favorites" cookbook using bookmap in Figure 7. We've added frontmatter to contain our copyright notice. We've also inserted "Cookies" as an explicit chapter element.

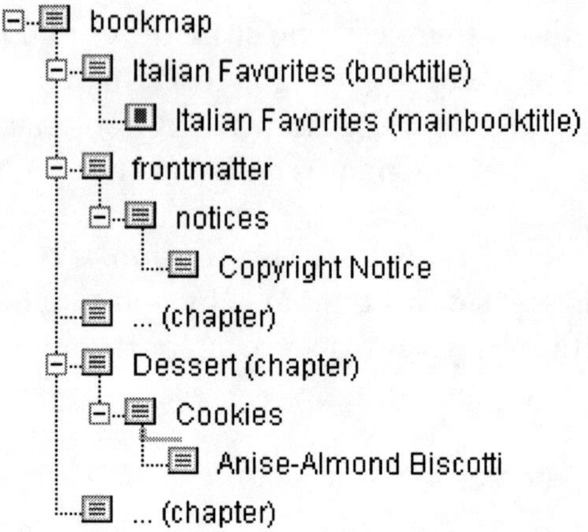

Figure 7: Italian Favorites cookbook implemented in bookmap

A day in the life of a DITA author

We're not going to cover the *whole* day, but we would like to discuss some of the ways that DITA changes writing projects.

Approaches to planning and developing content in DITA

The first thing you need to do is to think differently about the content you create. Don't think purely in terms of the output, as in "we create customer materials in different configuration to meet different needs." Instead, approach the content from this perspective: you create a library of content from which you can assemble and publish marketing materials to meet different needs. As one of our colleagues on the Enterprise Business Documents subcommittee of the DITA Technical Committee put it:

> *I see the creation of content and the creation of user deliverables as two separate tasks in topic-based authoring.*

Using maps as an outlining tool

Using a new technology does not mean stopping all of the tried and true tasks of content development. They might just look a little different. The process of developing an outline is one of those tasks.

Whether you are using traditional DTP tools rather than XML tools, an outline of the information product needs to be created. It doesn't matter if it's a Help system, a user guide, or a business report that needs to be created. Best practice is to create a comprehensive outline before starting to write. However, we recommend that when you move to DITA, you create outlines in a ditamap. After all, a ditamap is very close to an outline in form and function.

Approach the outline process as usual. Start from the outside with the big divisions and delve deeper to complete the outline. While developing the outline, look for topics to reuse. Add them to the map as they are found. Create new topics for outline headings that have not been written yet.

This is particularly beneficial for collaborative authoring. One of our clients, who creates technical manuals, has defined their process as follows:

- Each manual has a single owner. That owner is ultimately responsible for the PDF that will be delivered to a customer.
- At the start of a project, the owner is responsible for determining the requirements and establishing the authoring plan for the book.
- The owner then develops a ditamap for the book, selecting topics to reuse as appropriate and creating empty "stub" topics for each new topic that must be created.
- The owner writes the shortdesc for each stub topic to provide a clear overview of what the topic must contain when written.
- The stub topics are then assigned to authors in the group to be researched and completed.
- The owner is the only one who can edit the map, so if authors feel there are gaps or other issues in the map, they raise the issue with the owner and negotiate any changes.

What is a topic

Authors transitioning from traditional DTP tools and non-structured authoring frequently wrestle with the question "What is a topic?" Help authors usually do not have this sort of problem, as the approach to creating Help systems is topic-based. But authors who are accustomed to writing user guides or reports and are moving to DITA wrestle with the problem, especially when they are deciding how to move legacy content into DITA. From the technical document perspective, we sometimes describe a topic as a single answer to a single question. This works well for Help and reference guides. For example... How do I create an email address? What is an email address? What is the syntax of the print statement? These all fit the one question, one answer and one topic idea well.

Consider the first page of a new chapter. On it, you usually find a chapter title, a short description of the chapter and a list of the sections in the chapter. This still fits the one question, one answer and one topic idea. The type of topic is a navigation topic; it answers the question, "What is this chapter about?"

In business documents which frequently use a more narrative form of content presentation, the lines are blurred a bit. Some situations call for a "section" topic that really corresponds to a hierarchical perspective of heading levels, rather than more semantic structures.

Here are some guidelines to help determine how to most effectively write a topic:

- It should consist of only one subject. This does not mean you cannot have a few sub-sections in it, but keep it to one subject.
- It must stand on its own. This means that the topic can be read without the need to read any preceding or following information to understand it. It can be linked to other sections, but it needs to be complete unto itself.
- Keep it short. Think about reading the topic online. It will be an HTML page or Help topic. Nobody wants to scroll through pages and pages of information. And short topics in print are also more readable.
- Write it so that it can be reused. This means that it needs to be written so that it is not specific to any one usage (e.g., product, audience). When there is a need to differentiate the topic, think about using filtered reuse to handle the variations.

As a general rule, fall back on this:

- one concept topic documents one concept
- one task topic documents one task
- one reference topic provides one structural description, or one lookup table, or so on.

Writing structured content

Now you know what constitutes a topic, the only thing left to do is write your structured topics. Your organization should put in place best practices writing guidelines for how to create your content.

For example, writing guidelines for our recipes could look like Figure 1.

Recipe task	
task	
title	Mandatory. Capitalize each word in the title.
shortdesc	Mandatory. Create a short, one or two sentence introduction to the recipe that entices the reader to read on.
taskbody	
prereq	
table	
tablegroup	Mandatory. Use a two or three column table for the ingredients. The left column should contain quantity and measure, and the right column should contain the ingredient.If you need both imperial and metric measures, use the third column for metric. No column labels should be used when only imperial measures are used and are optional when using both measures.
context	Optional. Use context for tips, hints, background information.
steps	
step	
cmd	Mandatory. A cmd must always contain the condition under which the step is performed (e.g., in a medium sized bowl), followed by the action (e.g., mix together the first three ingredients).
result	Mandatory. The result contains the yield and nutritional ingredients.
p	Mandatory. Makes "X"servings.
p	Mandatory. Per serving:
ul	
li	Mandatory. Identify the number of calories in a single serving.
li	Mandatory. Identify the amount of protein in a single serving.
li	Mandatory. Identify the amount of fat in a single serving.

Figure 1: Writing guidelines for a recipe based on a DITA task.

Writing structured content simply means writing to a given structure. Instead of having to figure out how you want to organize and construct your content, you already have a plan. Think of it like a house. A house uses blueprints to ensure that the house will be built correctly. However, you still have full flexibility in how you design the interiors. With structured writing, you follow a plan which frees you up to focus on what's really important: the content, the usability and the most effective way of communicating the information. In many ways, writing structured content is easier than writing regular content because it allows you to focus on what's important rather than focusing on structure and appearance.

Planning for DITA

Even though DITA fits well into most technical documentation groups and many training groups, content cannot just be taken and imported into DITA. There are a number of steps to go through before getting up and running.

The plan

So many people look for the tools first, then say "OK, let's pour our content in." Unfortunately that does not result in a successful project. Instead:

- Begin with an awareness of your content and reuse requirements.
- Develop a unified content strategy.
- Identify your tools requirements (see "DITA and technology" on page 73)
- Convert your content.
- Train people.
- Implement.

Content analysis

It's critical to begin with an understanding of the content because only with an understanding of the content can the current state of the content be determined. You have to ask the following questions: How well is it structured? How consistent is it? And, what are the opportunities for reuse?

When performing a content analysis, review materials for content that is identical, similar, and unique. Take a representative sample of the content and analyze it for reuse. You can learn a lot about your content with analysis. Look for:

- Identical content - Identical content is content that is absolutely identical (wording, tense, capitalization, punctuation). Identical content can be easily reused. However, many times that content is almost, but not quite identical. This is similar content.
- Similar content - Similar content is content that is very similar to another piece of content. It may only vary by a few words, tense,

punctuation, layout, etc. When looking at similar content, determine if the differences are valid. Sometimes the differences are not really necessary and content could be identical. This is often found when content is copied and pasted and minor changes have been made, or if multiple people write the same thing, when it really could have been written once and reused many times.

- Unique - Content which is unique is just that, unique. It does not occur elsewhere in the information suite. It's specific to the product/service etc. being written about and is a necessary component of effective information.

Physical analysis vs. programmatic analysis of reuse

A software application which identifies the content that is identical and similar in the information set can be used. The software goes through the information set and identifies matching strings, passages and whole sections of content. It generates reports that provide a clear indication of reuse and enables you to look at the reuse that was identified.

We like to do a hands-on physical analysis of content because it provides us and the client with a really clear understanding of the state of their content. But we also like to do a programmatic analysis because it gives us a number we can use for ROI and provides an understanding of every opportunity for reuse.

Developing a unified content strategy

DITA is not just about structured writing and its not just about reuse, when you move to DITA you are moving to a methodology that emphasizes reuse, collaborative authoring, and a library of content, not documents. This calls for a unified content strategy to define how you will work. A unified content strategy is a plan of action to unify (bring together) content in a definitive source for optimum delivery to your customers. For more on a unified content strategy see our book *Managing Enterprise Content: A Unified Content Strategy*. Without a unified content strategy, DITA is just another way to create content, there is no value added to your content.

As part of the unified content strategy, determine "what's going on" with your content, how it's being used, how it's being managed, as well as the processes used to create, publish, and store it. Not surprisingly, these processes will vary across the organization.

Once you see how the information is being used and reused, you can decide how to unify it.

Define:

- how content should be structured for every information product (e.g., Help, manual)
- how the elements of the information products will be written (e.g., shortdesc, examples)
- where content will be reused (across information products, across content areas, across media)
- who will create what content when (who is responsible for creating the source and who is allowed to modify the source)

A unified content strategy also involves people and unified (collaborative) processes. The unified processes must create a collaborative environment in which authors throughout the organization can contribute to and draw content from a definitive source of information. Collaboration ensures that the content elements are consistent and can be reused wherever they are required. Processes should be redesigned to match the unified content strategy and support the way the authors work. Workflow can be used to support these processes.

Roles and responsibilities

Working with DITA is all about collaborative authoring. In a collaborative writing environment, authors work together to create a document set. Collaborative authoring is required in a unified content strategy to ensure content can be reused across many different areas and across many different types of documentation and media.

The traditional concept of ownership changes in a collaborative writing environment. While in the past a author may have been responsible for a particular document or a set of documentation, a author may now be responsible for creating content for a set of common topics that appear across documents. The author may no longer own the content for a whole document; the author may be responsible for a piece or a cross-section of a series of documents.

So, while an author still "owns" a particular element of information in the sense that he/she is the creator of the content and should be the only person who changes that content, the author actually has joint ownership with everyone else responsible for creating the information set.

The lack of complete ownership of content can be frustrating for an author. Authors may feel that the value of their contribution is diminished because they cannot specifically point to a complete information product. However, like an athletic team that shows pride and joy in a team win, so can authors.

In addition, when authors are required to use content written by other authors, they often exhibit the "not invented here syndrome." Sometimes people find it hard to believe that content somebody else created could possibly meet their needs. After all, it was written for a different purpose and media, and the author could not possibly know their customer/audience/requirements. In addition, other authors may have a different style. To resolve this issue, work with your authors to develop a common style and ensure that they understand and appreciate everyone's contribution.

Managers also feel they "own" the content associated with their area. It can be difficult for a product manager to understand and work with other product managers to ensure the consistency of content across information products. Managers need to be educated to understand the issues of differentiating content. Point out the costs of differentiation; more time to write, more time to edit and review, and if your organization translates content, the huge cost of translating all these different elements of information. When you are dealing with multiple requirements, it helps to have a content coordinator who can negotiate the unified content requirements and negotiate consensus with the product managers.

To help authors adopt collaborative writing techniques, involve authors in the analysis and design process and teach them conflict resolution skills. Involving authors in the analysis and design process will help them see the commonality in the work they do with the work that others do, and it will help them to work towards a shared understanding of content. Conflict is inevitable, especially in the early design phase and in the early adoption phase. Organizations need to recognize this and train people to deal with it.

We often get asked how much XML and DITA people need to know. In the early days of DITA everyone, including the authors really had to know XML and DITA, not so now. Today the tools have matured to a point where much of the "guts" of DITA can be hidden from the authors; however, they do need to understand the concepts of DITA at the level presented in this book. Someone who understands the technical details of DITA will be required to be your DITA technologist/systems administrator, but only they need to understand the intricacies of the technology under the surface.

The following describes some of the new and modified roles that are required in a DITA-based unified content strategy.

Content Coordinator (new)

Working in DITA means working in a collaborative environment. With a collaborative environment, someone needs to understand all of the content and the overall content requirements to ensure that content comes together in a logical manner. This task falls to a content coordinator (CC) to work with each of the product managers and the documentation and training groups to ensure that the unified content strategy is effectively addressed. This is a management role. In particular, the CC needs to communicate the concepts and advantages of reuse on an ongoing basis to facilitate agreement among project teams.

The content coordinator must also be able to oversee many projects and determine the unified content strategy required to address both the needs of all the product managers and the need of the content as a whole.

In addition, the CC must work with all the content creation teams to ensure models and guidelines are followed and everyone is in agreement on how to most effectively support the unified content strategy.

Skills and knowledge required include:

- a broad-based understanding of business needs
- the ability to determine an effective unified content strategy
- an in-depth understanding of customer needs and the ways in which the unified content strategy can support those needs
- an in-depth understanding of the unified content life cycle and the authors' requirements for success
- the ability to manage diverse requirements
- negotiating techniques
- strong people management skills

This role is primarily a management role with extensive coordination of people, processes and change, and a desire to implement and manage best practices.

Information Architect (new)

Information architects play a key role in analyzing and designing content. They are responsible for building the information product models, element models, metadata, reuse strategies, and determining appropriate specializations of DITA. They may also be responsible for designing the information retrieval for both authors and users. Accordingly, they should have a keen ability to design information for ease of use by content users and ease of reuse by authors.

The information architect needs the following skills:

Analysis

- analytical problem-solving
- information analysis
- content organizational analysis

Design

- information product and element models
- metadata
- user interface
- information retrieval
- reuse strategy
- reuse architecture and governance

Standards

- usability
- information

DITA Technologist (new)

In a traditional authoring system, many authors are responsible for creating the multiple media output for their content. However, in a DITA environment, the XML and associated issues such as specialization and stylesheets requires someone who knows and understands XML and DITA. We have rarely found this skill set in IT. A DITA technologist is required to handle the technology of the system. A manager needs to augment the team with this skill set.

An information technologist is skilled at implementing DITA in the various tools, including programming and supporting stylesheets to meet specifications provided by the information architect.

Information technologists should be well-versed in a wide variety of tools and technologies, including XML. Specifically, they should understand the tools and technologies chosen for the system.

Skills required include:

- DTDs
- authoring and publishing stylesheets
- DITA specializations
- workflow
- repository design

Authors (modified role)

DITA separates the creation of the input (content) from the output (media or information type). This means that authors (authors), as proficient communicators, will now rely less on the tools that are used to display the final information.

Authors no longer have to worry about applying formatting styles or becoming involved in the formatting of the information; formatting is automatically handled by the authoring and delivery systems. Instead, authors can concentrate exclusively on the content they create and combine.

Authors identify the building blocks of information and how the blocks will fit together. They also identify opportunities for content reuse and write applicable content elements for reuse.

Content Owners (modified role)

In a traditional writing environment, authors own the content they create because they are also responsible for creating a specific information product. However, in a unified content strategy, content can be used in many different information products. The concept of the content owner needs to change to accommodate this.

In a unified content strategy, the person who writes the content still owns it; however, they may not own all the content that comes together to create an information product. There may be many authors, all of whom may not be responsible for creating an entire information product. Rather, they may be responsible for creating content about a certain subject that goes into many different information products.

In addition, there needs to be an owner of the unified content, someone who can oversee the creation of all the content related to a particular product, service, product family, or any other associated content set. The unified content owner facilitates the collaborative authoring process and ensures consistency and quality of the materials. This could be a team leader.

Editors (modified role)

Standards and consistency are important in creating seamless unified materials. In a unified content environment, it's particularly important that editors not just look at the words, but look at how the information is used to ensure it is written effectively for reuse.

The editors will be able to focus on the effectiveness of the content since many of the issues they now address such as use of boilerplate and stylesheets will be automated.

Content conversion

We often get asked about converting content. The ease of the conversion is only as good as the quality of the content to begin with. If the authors were consistent in how they created content and content used templates there is a good chance that the content can be converted programmatically, but sadly that is usually not the case.

We do not recommend converting all of the content. Rather, convert the content in phases as and when the content needs to be updated. It is worthwhile talking to a company that specializes in conversion as they can typically convert content very rapidly and at a reasonable cost.

Training and consulting

No implementation should occur without adequate training of all staff. Training should always be part of the investment costs.

An organization may be able to implement a DITA-based unified content strategy on its own without help from consultants for information analysis, specializations, software installation and configuration, and change management. However, most organizations use some level of consulting either from the tools vendors or from other consultants in information design and management, and change management.

We recommend:

- The DITA technologist take all the available training from the vendor (user, installation and configuration, stylesheets).
- The use of consultants to facilitate the process of information analysis, content modeling, metadata and workflow. While this type of support is available from a vendor, they are focused on the tool and do not necessarily truly understand content and your business.
- The consultant provide knowledge transfer training to ensure you can support your own requirements long term.
- The structured authoring training to authors be separate from the tool training. Trying to teach structured writing at the same time as teaching someone to use a tool often results in the key aspects of the concepts of structured writing getting mired in the "mechanics." Think of it like learning to drive a standard car vs. learning to drive, then applying this skill set to a standard car, so much easier and more effective!
- Once the authors have a grasp of structured writing, provide tools training.

Metadata

Metadata is a topic that is often overlooked in technical documentation; many companies moving to DITA don't use the metadata provided. However, metadata is very important to an effective unified content strategy and is critical when working in a content management system.

What is metadata and why is it important?

What is metadata? The typical answer is that it's "data about data." Although that's true, it's not a particularly enlightening answer.

So what's so important about metadata?

Metadata is the glue that enables the system (and by extension, you) to find the information you need. It's the "stuff" that allows computers to be "smart." It's the stuff that makes "intelligent content" intelligent. And when it's missing or poorly implemented, it's what makes us slap the side of the computer in frustration when we can't find what we're looking for.

Let's take a look at the most common metadata that most people are familiar with, at least at a superficial level – the metadata used by Microsoft Office.

Open a Word file and look in the Files > Properties location. Click on the General Tab and a box like the one below appears.

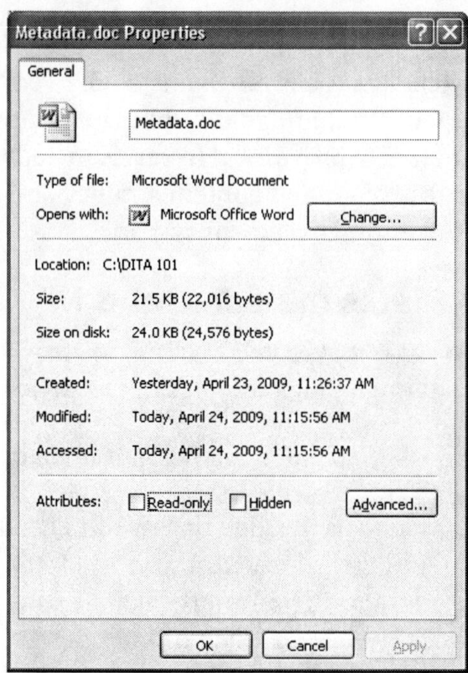

Figure 1: Metadata properties General tab

It contains information about the file just opened such as its name, when it was created, where it is located, etc. Now, close the file and hover over the name in the File Manager. Some of that same information (name, date modified and size) will be displayed in the hover box.

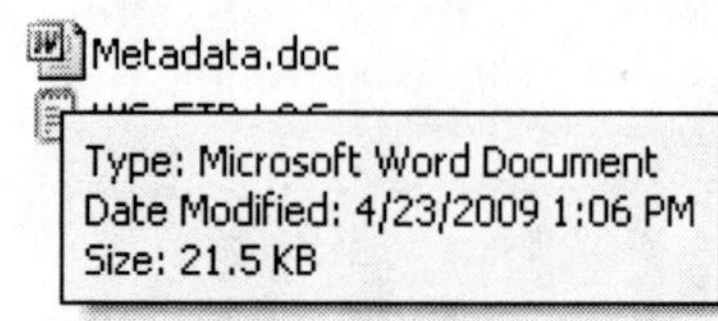

Figure 2: Hover box showing metadata

Right click on the filename and select Properties from the options presented. More information is displayed, such as where the file is located, when it was created (in addition to its last modification) and other details.

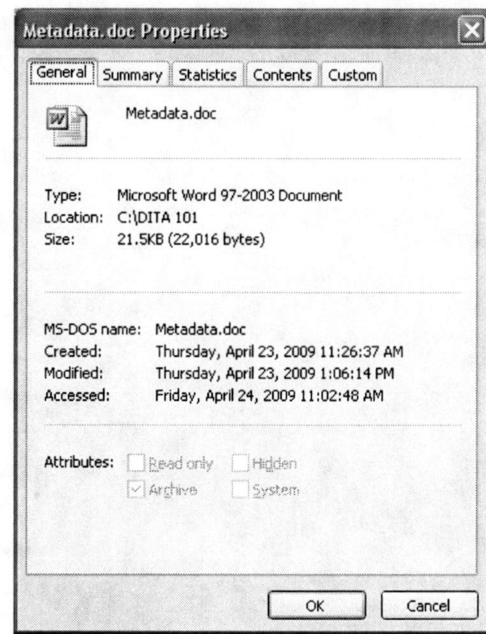

Figure 3: Properties box from File Manager, showing metadata

All this information is metadata. It allows you to know more about the file in question. On a Windows system, the metadata helps the search tool find particular files. This information is very generic though; by adding your own metadata to a file, it becomes more useful to you.

Reopen that Word file and once again navigate to the Properties dialog box. Select the Summary tab this time and you will see a window where you can enter your own information.

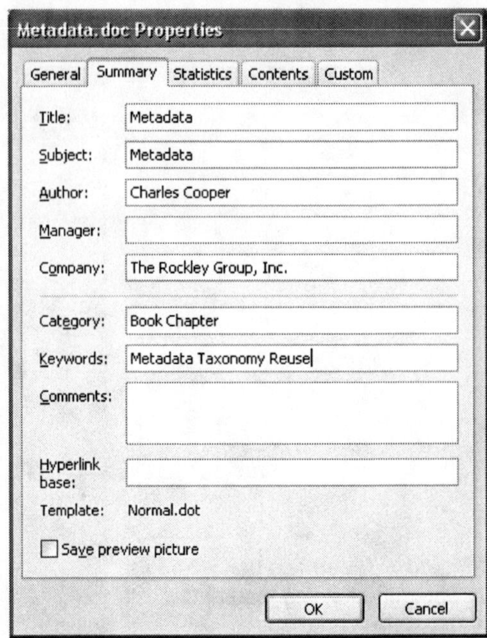

Figure 4: Metadata properties, Summary tab

Enter some information there (the Author's name, the Subject, Keywords and other information is entered in the example) and close the file. Once again, hover over the file name in Explorer to see a bit more information about what is contained in the file – even without opening it.

Figure 5: Hover box showing additional metadata

In Word though, it's the Custom Tab that shows the power that metadata can bring to content. On the Properties dialog box, select the Custom tab to open the scroll box containing a number of possible types of metadata, including Checked By, Department, Disposition, etc. Any of these can be selected and relevant information entered there. In the world of content management, this is known as Tagging.

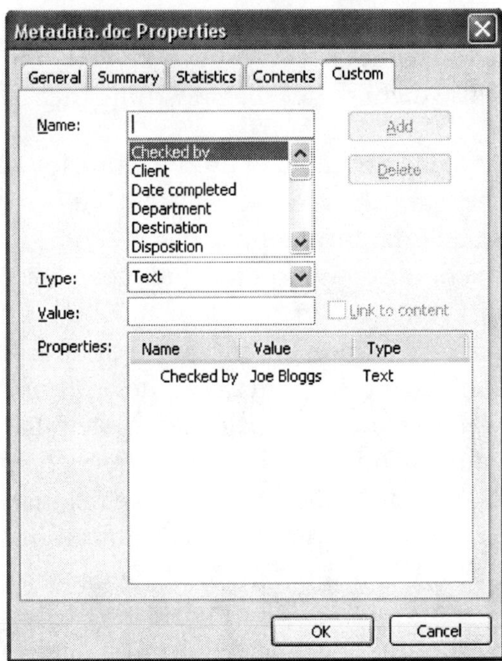

Figure 6: Metadata properties, Custom tab

The file can be tagged with the name of the reviewer (in this case, Joe Bloggs), the date the file was reviewed and a host of other information. Any program that can read this information can use it to narrow searches and help find information being looked for. For example, if you are looking for a particular file and you know that Joe Bloggs reviewed it (rather than Jill), you can search for any Word file reviewed by Joe and that is all the search engine will look for.

The real strength of metadata only comes when *all* the information available is tagged in a similar manner. If everyone in an organization tagged information in the same way, then they could build on that shared knowledge and find information across the organization with the help of the embedded metadata. Word files, spreadsheets, images, movies and more can be tagged for retrieval. This way all Word files that Joe had reviewed are found, not just searcher's files that he reviewed.

However, it's when the contents of those files (the components that they are made of) are tagged, that information can not only be found, but reused throughout a department or organization.

This enables the content creators to find individual components and reuse them rather than rewriting them.

Imagine a number of product lines for audio components in which all the manuals (across the product lines) were supposed to contain standard information about the company. If an audit was conducted, the findings would probably show that the "standard" content was different from manual to manual. And if each line was supposed to have a common description about the product, the findings would show that those "common" descriptions varied as well. If you were using a content management system to manage the content, you could identify that common company information with a tag, ensure that it was "built into" all of the manuals and ensure that the product line specific common descriptions were built into each of the product lines. And because of the tagging, the correct product line descriptions could be matched with the product lines. For example, the headphone descriptions would be built into the headphone materials and the loudspeaker descriptions would be made available in the speaker materials – and not vice versa.

Prolog Metadata in DITA

In a DITA implementation, the built-in metadata tagging fields seen within Word or similar programs are not usually used. DITA has its own metadata structures that are used instead. For a complete list of prolog metadata in DITA (the metadata that can appear in the prolog section at the top of a topic), see "Appendix B - Prolog Metadata" on page 107.

In DITA, the prolog section of a file carries metadata about that file. The information can contain the author's name, the date the file was created or modified, any keywords that the author wants to add and a host of other things.

DITA organizes its metadata into three broad sub-categories, publication metadata, management metadata and qualification metadata.

Publication metadata

Publication metadata is designed to provide information about the topic as a publication.

These include:

- author – the person or organization who creates the content
- publisher – the person or organization who distributes the content
- copyright – the copyright and licensing information about the content

Management metadata

Management metadata is concerned with providing the type of information needed to manage the content within a workflow system. The workflow system has ability to read this metadata and act on it. Depending on the system, it might have the ability to change and update the management metadata.

The management metadata includes:

- source – an identifier or reference to the source material for the content
- critdates – critical dates in the management cycle that can include specific dates (content created, approved or published) or date spans (review cycle)
- permissions – defines the "security" that content has such as the level of entitlement that a user or system must have to get access to the content
- resourceid – a unique identifier assigned to each topic and used for system management purposes

Qualification metadata

Qualification metadata provides "background" or supporting information about a topic. They may be used by a content management and workflow system to process the information. Qualification metadata can be applied at many levels. It may be applied to an individual topic and may also be used in a Topic Map to multiple topics. When a particular element is used in both a topic and a topic map, the topic map information is regarded as more important and will take precedence over the individual topic information.

Qualification metadata includes:

- audience – This defines the intended audience for the topic and includes the type, job and the experience level of the reader. For example, the audience for a topic could be defined as a programmer, who would be programming (rather than managing or administering) with an expert experience level.
- category – This provides a simple method of organizing the topics by category. In order to maintain efficiency and accuracy, the categories should be predefined and made into a controlled vocabulary for tagging. Topics can belong to multiple categories.
- keywords – These are words that are specifically designed to help find the content or topic. They are often best chosen from a controlled vocabulary to maximize accuracy and efficiency.
- prodinfo – This is a simple definition of the product (or platform, in the case of software) that the particular topic is related to.
- othermeta – It is used to identify and define properties that do not fit into other metadata. It allows the metadata to be tailored to specific needs and does away with the need to have a "miscellaneous" tag.
- data – Primarily used as a base for specialized metadata structures and allows for complex nesting metadata information.

Selection attributes

Selection attributes are metadata that are applied to the elements within a topic that supports conditional processing of the content such as how we choose to show or hide information so that it can be incorporated into (or excluded from) a publishing process.

DITA 1.0 limits conditional processing to a select few metadata attributes (audience, platform, product and otherprops). Future versions of DITA will allow users to define their own selection attributes.

audience – This defines the intended audience for the element. For example the audience for our recipes could be novice, experienced and professional.

platform – This identifies the operating system and/or hardware required to support a particular program.

product – This defines the product (e.g., hardware or software) the content applies to.

otherprops – otherprops (other properties) is sort of a miscellaneous "bucket" for metadata. In other words, it allows you to have other values for filtering the content like "healthy" and "regular" we used in the recipes.

Relationship to other types of metadata (Dublin Core)

Much of the DITA metadata relates very closely to the standard categories of the Dublin Core Metadata Initiative. This ensures that the information included in the file is readable by many types of applications (e.g., Enterprise Content Management Systems). The Dublin Core Metadata includes types such as Contributor (a person, team, department or other organization who contributed to a piece of information), Creator (a person, team, department or other organization who created a piece of information) and Format (definition of whatever format is best used to describe piece of information – size, weight, length or time).

Metadata in taxonomy

The word taxonomy covers a lot of ground. A taxonomy is a system of organizing information so that it can be found. Implementing taxonomies require a series of tools and techniques such as Controlled Vocabularies, Synonym Rings and Authority Lists, Thesauri and, of course, Metadata. Controlled Vocabularies define the words and forms we will use; Synonym Rings and Authority Lists define what words are similar to each other; and Thesauri define the relationships between the words. Metadata ties it all together.

When we implement metadata for taxonomy use, we tend to divide it into two main types: categorization metadata and element metadata. Categorization metadata is often used by end users to find information, as it separates the information into categories (known as facets to taxonomy nerds). Element metadata tends to be more granular and focuses on the individual elements of content. Element metadata helps authors find information so that it can be reused in different documents or for different purposes. We break down the element metadata into three sub-categories. Metadata for reuse, metadata for retrieval and metadata for tracking.

Metadata for reuse is used to identify content components that can be used in multiple locations. For example, if a product had a series of headphones, you would probably have an overview that describes the product line. That overview could appear in a manual, in the Help, on the Web, etc. To make it easy to find and reuse, you could tag the content with "content type = overview, product = headphones." This would enable the right overview for the right line of products to be found.

Metadata for Retrieval is used to help find information based on typical "human centric" search criteria. These include the document title, the author or reviewer or date published. This might also include keywords (for the line of headphones that might include bass boost, headphones, DJ, etc.)

Element metadata typically includes tracking or status metadata that a CMS uses to manage the content within it. This includes such elements as various dates (created, reviewed, edited, saved, published, archived), user activity (creator, reviewer, publisher) and status (first draft, second draft, in review, published, obsolete), etc.

Metadata and your content management system

Metadata is the lifeblood of a content management system. It is used to identify, track and manage all of the content within the system. Just as importantly, it uses metadata to link to the "outside world" of authors, managers, reviewers, publishers, etc.

A content management system serves two main purposes: managing the actual content and managing the content through the workflow. Workflow is the automated process that carries the information from the author, through the review/edit cycle and onto publishing. In pre-automation days, the same processes took place, but often involved literally carrying typed or printed copies of documents from one person to another. Once email became routine, files were emailed from person to person, speeding up the process, but it was still a piecemeal affair and subject to error.

Old versions of a file might be sent, information might be sent to the wrong person, a file might be sent "for immediate review" to someone who was on holiday – or no longer with the company. At each step of the process, control of the information was lost and the status of that information could only be guessed at.

By automating the workflow, a content management system can provide automatic status information about any piece of information it is tracking. With a manual system, the author might know that they sent a particular file to a particular reviewer, but would not know if the reviewer actually looked at the file until they asked – or the return data had passed. With a content management system, the author could know that the reviewer had received the file, had opened it (or not) and maybe even what work the reviewer had done on it. If the reviewer was not in the office, the system could forward it to a secondary reviewer and the author would have been notified of the change.

All of this is possible due to a properly constructed workflow. When it is properly implemented, it can seem like magic. So much so, that we often refer to workflow happening "automagically." It's not magic – it's just workflow driven (in part) by metadata.

The metadata defines the author and the reviewers. It defines alternates for reviewers. It defines anyone who will ever touch the content, be "they" an individual, a department, an ad hoc group, or a content management system or publishing system.

By knowing "who everyone" is, and by tracking when and how they interact with the content, the changing status of any particular piece of information can be managed.

DITA and technology

Almost all XML-based or structure-based tools now support DITA. While you could do DITA using non-structured tools, we don't recommend it. DITA tools provide a whole lot of functionality to make authoring, managing and delivering DITA-based content a whole lot easier. Using DITA without a supporting tool requires either working in raw XML code, not something anybody wants to do on a regular basis, or it means having to be very consistent and rigorous in following the DITA structure, because the existing tools won't enforce DITA structures.

The following provides a top-level understanding of the kind of functionality to look for in these tools. For a more detailed understanding of DITA tools and key differentiators see our CMS Watch *XML & Component Content Management Report 2009* (http://www.cmswatch.com/CCM/Report/).

Authoring

Moving to DITA is a big change for authors. Moving to structured authoring and XML is a pretty significant shift. Make it easier for your authors by selecting the right authoring tool.

Will you need a new authoring tool for authors? Probably. At the very least, the existing authoring tool will need to be used differently. (For example, FrameMaker users might switch from using FrameMaker in unstructured mode to structured mode.) It's more likely that you'll need to buy new authoring tools for your authors.

The key features to look for in an authoring tool are:

- the authoring interface
- text handling capabilities
- DITA support

We'll explain in a little more detail.

The authoring interface

When you select tools, make sure first and foremost that the tool will be right for the people who will be using it; the authors. This means that you might need to stay away from the fun and fancy for the plain and effective. The cool technology that exposes the full depth of functionality of XML and DITA could be less effective for your users than the simple tool with limited functionality. You must match the interface to the needs of the people who will be using it.

One of the first characteristics that can affect usability of an authoring tool is the degree to which it can hide (or expose) the guts of DITA and XML from the authors. If they are used to authoring content in MS Word, then you'll probably need to find a tool that hides as much XML and DITA terminology and complexity, along with the XML markup, as possible. If you're providing a tool for authors who have long experience in other markup languages (like SGML) or in Help Authoring Tools, then you might be able to expose them to more DITA and XML without too much trouble. You may want to ensure that authors get to choose whether they see the complexities or not; there are many authoring tools that provide multiple views of content so users can select to see tags or not.

Text handling capabilities

It's also important to remember that you're selecting a authoring tool and there are certain things that authors expect in such a tool. Spell checkers and grammar checkers. Change bars. Table wizards. Graphics preview, etc. When surveying our clients' authors to find out what sort of functionality they feel is most important, spell checkers are always near the top.

Try to provide the authors the same sort of or similar authoring features to what they have now. They will get over that whole need to enter tags rather than formats, but they'll be disappointed if the basic features that help them to craft text are missing.

DITA support

We used to warn people to be wary of the potentially empty promise from tool vendors: "We support DITA." Why? Because any tool that supports XML can support DITA. All you have to do is load the

DTDs. Then you can say you have DITA support, but it's not really as effective as it could be.

Today, tool vendors have found that they cannot compete for any share of the DITA authoring market unless they go beyond simply bundling DITA DTDs or schemas and provide specific functional support for the various features of DITA. Some features to look for include:

- Rules validation – First and foremost, an authoring tool that will validate content against the DITA standard, guide the authors through the tag entry process and ensure that the author cannot break the structure rules in tagging is needed.
- Map editor – All authoring tools can create topics, but you want to make sure they can also create and maintain maps. You will want the ability to easily add topicrefs (maybe by drag and drop), move them around and add metadata to the maps.
- Conref/Linking/Xref interface – Early editors required that the author enter link targets by typing hrefs directly. Make sure that your authoring tool makes it easy to create links of any sort by drag and drop, selecting from lists or from browsing a repository (file system or Component Content Management System [CCMS]) without having to type URLs/file names directly.
- Conditional text interface – Conditional text is potentially very powerful, but without the right tool, it can be difficult to work with. Make sure you can highlight conditional text, perhaps with color and filter out conditions so variants are seen.
- Publication interface – Unless DITA files are delivered to the end users, you will need to publish out to a different format. You may therefore need a publishing interface that can pass content and instructions to publishing tools (perhaps the DITA Toolkit) to create the output.

A final, but particularly important feature to consider is if the preferred authoring tool actually interfaces with the selected CCMS if you have one.

Component content management system (CCMS)

The question of whether a content management system is needed for DITA is essentially the same questions as asking if a content management system is needed at all. If you answer "yes" to most of the following questions, a CCMS may be appropriate.

- Do you have lots of authors (greater than 10)?
- Are your authors in multiple locations?
- Do you have a large content suite?
- Do you translate your content?

Component content management systems (CCMS) manage content at a granular (component) level of content, rather than at the page or document level. Each component represents a single topic, concept, or asset (such as an image or table). Components are assembled into multiple content assemblies (information products) and can be viewed as components or as traditional pages or documents. Each component has its own lifecycle (owner, version, approval, use) and can be tracked individually, or as part of an assembly. CCM is typically used for multichannel customer-facing content (marketing, usage, learning, support). CCM can be a separate system or a functionality of another content management type (such as an Enterprise Content Management System [ECM]). The technical documentation world is most often interested in a dedicated CCMS.

Dedicated systems were developed out of the technical documentation industry's requirement for multichannel publishing – first to print and Help, then to print, Help and Web, and now also to wireless and mobile devices. Component management was built into these systems not only to address the specific requirements of multiple channels, but more importantly, to address differences in product, platform, audience and content type. Many of these systems have existed for more than a decade, working first with SGML and now with XML and DITA.

All good content management systems, regardless of type, should provide strong facilities for security, check in/out, version control and robust access to information.

The key factors for a CCMS are:

- support for DITA
- support for reuse
- support for translation

Support for DITA

The biggest functionality in a CCMS where DITA is concerned is the ability to support DITA maps. A lot of vendors let the authoring tool handle maps, but if you really want to control and move the content around with ease, look for solid DITA map support in the CCMS. This allows users to easily look at the content suite and move content around at will.

Support for reuse

In one sense, support for DITA is support for reuse, but support for reuse can go beyond the traditional support in DITA and provide extensive support for reuse. Some areas to consider:

- Reports – Reports are really essential to managing reuse. Desirable reports include where used, percentage of reuse, potential reuse (e.g., content which is similar but not identical), derivative reuse (content which is reused, but then changed).
- Versioning – Versioning makes it possible to reuse different versions of content in different circumstances. For example, a product is using v.2 of three different topics and concurrently the same product is being prepared for the next release uses v.2 of two of the topics and v.3 of one of the topics. The author can select from a number of versions of a topic for inclusion.
- Filtered reuse (conditions) – Sometimes content uses simple conditions (1-5) to differentiate content for use in different situations, but content used in very complex situations (across regions, audiences, products) can become very complex and requires additional support. One of our clients could have up to 500 conditions for one topic!
- Updates – It is important to be able to decide how to update reusable content. It is valuable to have automated update (automatically updated when the source updates), notified update

(let me know that it is updated so I can decide to update or not), severed update (the reused content is no longer related to the source so no update occurs).

Support for translation

If the content is to be translated, you must have strong support for translation workflow including topics, maps and documents.

- Seamless workflow – Sometimes the translation workflow is outside of the organization and is very difficult to track, so the ability to hand off content from the creation/review/approval cycle directly to the workflow cycle is desirable.
- Integration with a translation memory tool – Pass the content directly to a translation memory system either internally or externally.
- Seamless re-integration of translated content – Reintegrate translated content back into the content management system for management and delivery.

Publishing

The author's job is usually not to deliver DITA topics. The author's job is to deliver a Help system, marketing brochure, training manual, etc. That means before delivering the content, it must be published out to a different format. Or, it might have to be delivered out to several formats, with different subsets of content. A publishing system might therefore need to be purchased to perform the conversion and output creation. Depending on the formats delivered, you might need two or more different systems.

Before we talk about the features to look for in a publishing tool, this is a good time to talk about the DITA Open Toolkit. You may not need a separate publishing tool if you are using DITA, because you can use the DITA Open Toolkit to publish. It's free, and does provide basic publication capabilities for print (PDF), Help, and Web.

That said, here are some things to consider:

- Supported formats – A key factor if the output is primarily HTML (whether as a Help variant or as loose HTML files for a Web site) is that the DITA Open Toolkit might be all that's required. But if the output is PDF, you have a more difficult choice to make. The PDF output capabilities of the Toolkit are improved, but you might need a commercial tool to do the fancier publishing.

- Stylesheets (standards-based or proprietary) – Since you are implementing XML, it may appear to make sense to use an XML-based stylesheet language like XSL. Maybe. While the transformation side of XSL is very solid and capable, it's generally agreed that it has not reached the same level of older style formats (like FOSI). Plus, some tools were created before XSL was available and use proprietary stylesheet formats.
- Interactive vs. batch – This is an area that many authors find hard to deal with when they move from traditional DTP to XML-based publishing. Most XML implementations use a batch-based publishing mechanism, where DITA source and stylesheets are fed into a rendering engine which spits out the required format at the other end. authors have limited (or no) ability to "tweak" the output for line-breaks or page breaks or so on. If this functionality is required, you'll need a tool that can ingest DITA content, render it on screen and allow you to tweak and tune (like DTP) to your heart's content. You will probably need to pay more for this functionality.
- Speed – Some publishing engines have created a market niche by providing fast, batch-based publishing, for example, for hundreds of thousands of pages per day. Speed is not usually a factor for most, but for business documents, it can be vital.

One last point: stylesheets are code. That is, they are more like a programming language than they are purely a stylesheet definition mechanism like cascading stylesheets (CSS). You might need to buy something to help you create stylesheets. More likely, you'll need to buy someone. Make sure there are some consulting dollars in the budget.

The "advanced" stuff

As you move beyond the basics of map/topic, you will find features of DITA that really help to extend the capabilities of structured authoring and reuse in DITA.

Domains

The official definition of a domain from the v1.0 DITA Architectural Specification is:

> *"A DITA domain defines a set of elements associated with a particular subject area or authoring requirement regardless of topic type."*

We're going to explain what domains are using an example from a project where we had to move from one markup language (TeX) to FrameMaker to document a software application. As part of the template design exercise, we analyzed the guides to identify all of the details of the interface that we wanted to identify using a different format in the guides. In this project, we made file names bold. So we decided that we needed a character style called filename. Field names on screens were also bold so we also created a character style called fieldname. These styles could be applied to file or field names in user guides, reference guides, or in any other type.

That's what domains are: they are specific sets of semantic elements used to document certain types of content. For example, if you are documenting a programming language or interface, there is a domain for you that includes elements for things like API name, parameter name and language syntax blocks.

What makes this useful, beyond providing the semantic elements for use, is the fact that by grouping the different elements by domain, it makes it easy to hide domains you don't want to use, or restrict domains to certain types of topics. For example, you can allow the programming domain in reference topics, but restrict it from conceptual topics.

The domains available in DITA include:

- indexing
- programming
- software
- typographic
- user interface
- utilities

For example, the elements in the user interface domain include:

- uicontrol - for button names, fields, menu items, or other interface objects
- wintitle - for window titles
- menucascade - or menu sequences (like File > New)
- shortcut - for keyboard or shortcuts
- screen - for screen descriptions

Conrefs

There are times when you might want to use a piece of a topic rather than the whole topic. It might be a paragraph or a series of paragraphs. It could even be a single word. We call this fragment reuse, see “Fragment-based reuse” on page 24.

This kind of reuse can be extremely effective. It’s used for things like notes, cautions and warnings. It’s also used for index keywords (a good idea for a standardized index).

What makes conrefs so powerful is that the fragment of text does not necessarily need to be a physically separate piece of content. Using conrefs, you can create a topic that reuses a single paragraph from another topic, without having to burst (break out/chunk) that paragraph out of the existing topic. This is potentially very useful. For example, you can create a single file of standardized index keywords and use the conref mechanism to insert them into any topic as necessary. This is a more effective alternative to saving each keyword as its own little chunk of content and reusing it.

One one word of warning: not all authoring tools or content management tools are capable of supporting the DITA standard for conrefs fully. That is, some systems still rely on bursting reusable fragments out into separately managed chunks of content to facilitate this sort of reuse.

Technology aside, conrefs can be very useful. As a practical example, compare the way the units are represented in the Couscous and the Cheesecake recipes. They’re not consistent. The couscous recipe refers to “teaspoons” and “tablespoons;” the cheesecake recipe refers to “tsp” and “tbl.” You can use conrefs to eliminate the inconsistency.

In this example, we first created a file to contain all the units we wanted (see Figure 1).

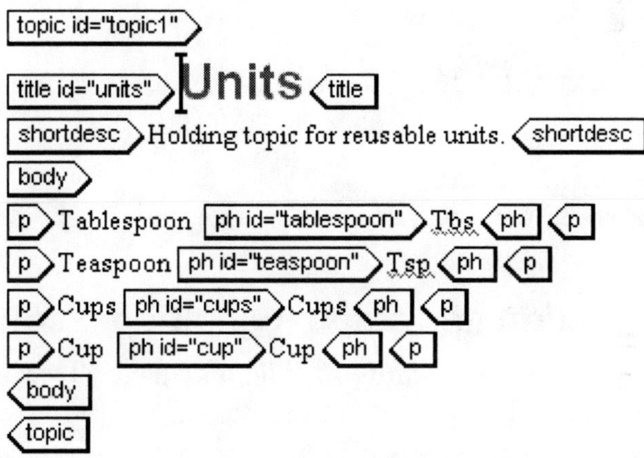

Figure 1: Units file with definitions of all the units of measure

Then we revised the Couscous recipe, replacing explicit units (Cup, teaspoon, etc.) with units conref’d from our units file. Next, we modify all of recipes the same way and ensure that all units are consistent.

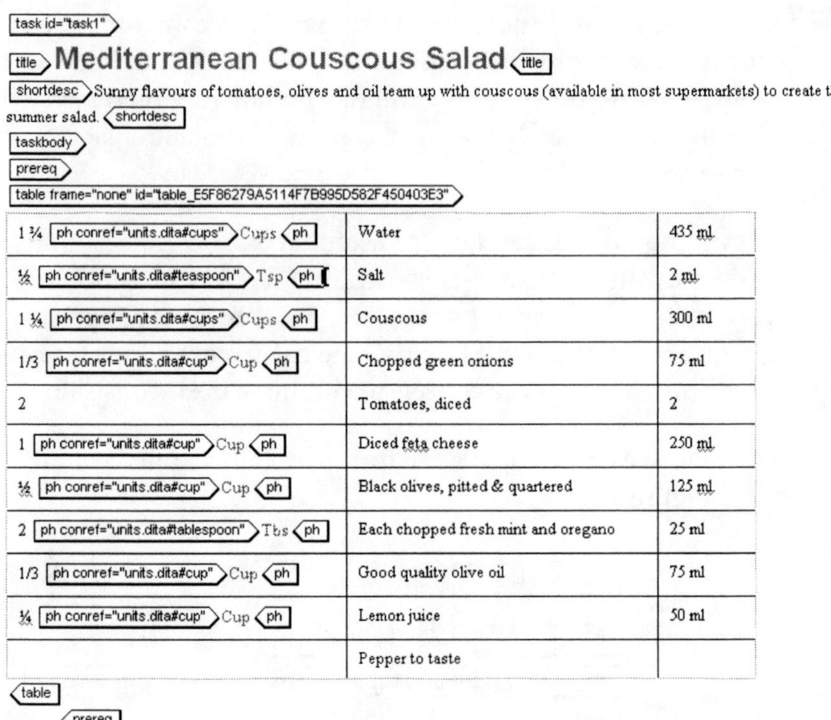

task id="task1"

title **Mediterranean Couscous Salad** title

shortdesc Sunny flavours of tomatoes, olives and oil team up with couscous (available in most supermarkets) to create this summer salad. shortdesc

taskbody

prereq

table frame="none" id="table_E5F86279A5114F7B995D582F450403E3"

1 ¾ ph conref="units.dita#cups" Cups ph	Water	435 ml
½ ph conref="units.dita#teaspoon" Tsp ph	Salt	2 ml
1 ¼ ph conref="units.dita#cups" Cups ph	Couscous	300 ml
1/3 ph conref="units.dita#cup" Cup ph	Chopped green onions	75 ml
2	Tomatoes, diced	2
1 ph conref="units.dita#cup" Cup ph	Diced feta cheese	250 ml
½ ph conref="units.dita#cup" Cup ph	Black olives, pitted & quartered	125 ml
2 ph conref="units.dita#tablespoon" Tbs ph	Each chopped fresh mint and oregano	25 ml
1/3 ph conref="units.dita#cup" Cup ph	Good quality olive oil	75 ml
¼ ph conref="units.dita#cup" Cup ph	Lemon juice	50 ml
	Pepper to taste	

table

prereq

Figure 2: Couscous recipe with units of measure inserted as conrefs

Selection attributes (conditional content)

Sometimes it's just not possible to manage all variations of content in individual little pieces. Sometimes information needs to be kept together, perhaps because the variations are very small and at other times because the context around it is needed to be able to create the content. Pieces of content that are very small can become a management nightmare. Conditional text allows variations in content (versions) to be kept in a single file, but filters out what isn't wanted when creating the outputs. See "Filtered reuse" on page 27 for more information.

In DITA, conditional processing support/filtered reuse is provided by selection attributes. DITA 1.0 limits conditional processing to a select few variants (platform, product, audience and otherprops), with future versions of DITA allowing users to define their own selection attributes.

For example, let's imagine that we need to create two versions of a recipe: the regular version and a dairy-free version. That means we need to replace butter with a margarine. We can add tagging to each reference of butter to identify that it belongs to the regular version. We'll also add margarine, tagged as dairy-free. We've used the "otherprops" attribute as in Figure 3).

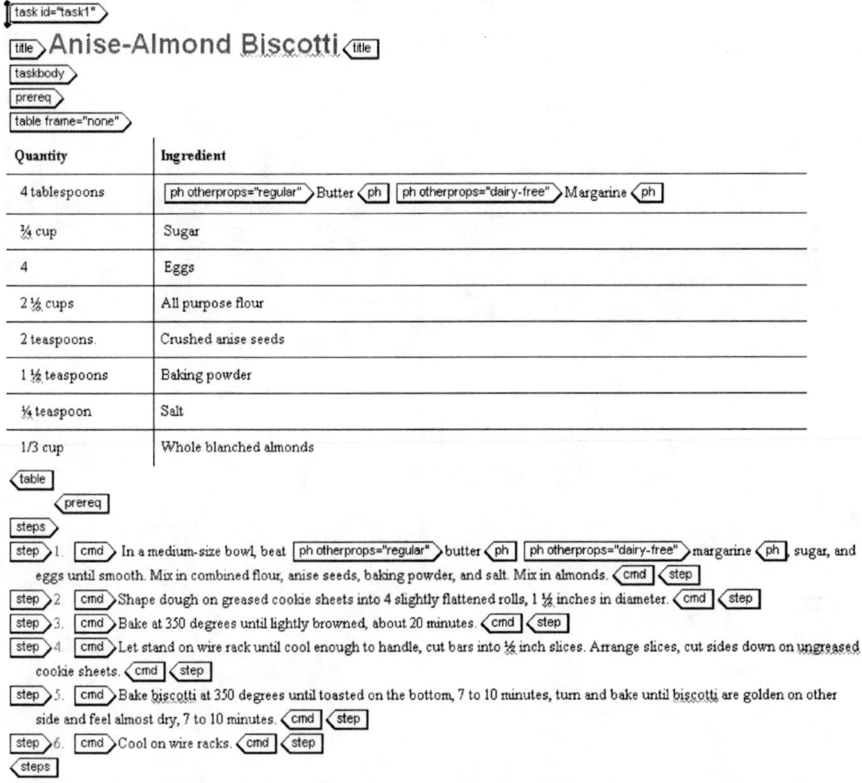
task id="task1"
title Anise-Almond Biscotti title
taskbody
prereq
table frame="none"

Quantity	Ingredient
4 tablespoons	ph otherprops="regular" Butter ph ph otherprops="dairy-free" Margarine ph
¾ cup	Sugar
4	Eggs
2 ½ cups	All purpose flour
2 teaspoons.	Crushed anise seeds
1 ½ teaspoons	Baking powder
¼ teaspoon	Salt
1/3 cup	Whole blanched almonds

table
prereq
steps
step 1. cmd In a medium-size bowl, beat ph otherprops="regular" butter ph ph otherprops="dairy-free" margarine ph, sugar, and eggs until smooth. Mix in combined flour, anise seeds, baking powder, and salt. Mix in almonds. cmd step
step 2. cmd Shape dough on greased cookie sheets into 4 slightly flattened rolls, 1 ½ inches in diameter. cmd step
step 3. cmd Bake at 350 degrees until lightly browned, about 20 minutes. cmd step
step 4. cmd Let stand on wire rack until cool enough to handle, cut bars into ½ inch slices. Arrange slices, cut sides down on ungreased cookie sheets. cmd step
step 5. cmd Bake biscotti at 350 degrees until toasted on the bottom, 7 to 10 minutes, turn and bake until biscotti are golden on other side and feel almost dry, 7 to 10 minutes. cmd step
step 6. cmd Cool on wire racks. cmd step
steps

Figure 3: Biscotti recipe with alternate ingredient for butter

This one topic can now be processed out to two different versions: dairy-free and regular. Using the otherprops attribute along with the functionality in editors or component content management systems, we can process this topic to create the necessary output. In Figure 4, we've selected the dairy-free version.

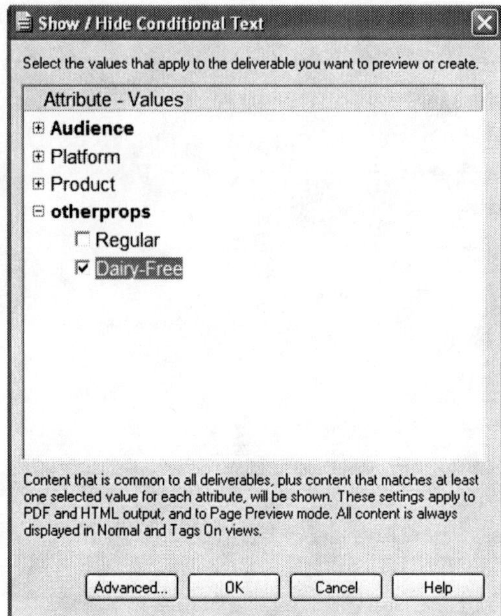

Figure 4: Selecting the dairy-free version in the conditional setting panel of my editor

The HTML output (Figure 5) shows the ingredient as "Margarine," appropriate for the dairy-free version.

Anise-Almond Biscotti

Quantity	Ingredient
4 tablespoons	Margarine
¾ cup	Sugar
4	Eggs
2 ½ cups	All purpose flour
2 teaspoons.	Crushed anise seeds
1 ½ teaspoons	Baking powder
¼ teaspoon	Salt
1/3 cup	Whole blanched almonds

1. In a medium-size bowl, beat margarine, sugar, and eggs until smooth. Mix in combined flour, anise seeds, baking powder, and salt. Mix in almonds.
2. Shape dough on greased cookie sheets into 4 slightly flattened rolls, 1 ½ inches in diameter.
3. Bake at 350 degrees until lightly browned, about 20 minutes.
4. Let stand on wire rack until cool enough to handle, cut bars into ½ inch slices. Arrange slices, cut sides down on ungreased cookie sheets.
5. Bake biscotti at 350 degrees until toasted on the bottom, 7 to 10 minutes, turn and bake until biscotti are golden on other side and feel almost dry, 7 to 10 minutes.
6. Cool on wire racks.

Figure 5: HTML output (with minimal formatting) of the dairy-free version of Biscotti

Selection attributes can be applied to almost any element, to conditionally process words, phrases, paragraphs, images, tables, or even topics.

Relationship tables

A relationship table (reltables) is a feature that helps manage related links better. Relationship tables are built-in map files and provide an alternative to building related topic references in individual topics themselves.

The advantage here is that the use of reltables makes it easier to ensure that you are not pointing to a topic that is not in the map or which is not included in the output. Equally important, if you add a new topic that is related to a dozen other topics, each of which should point to it as a related topic, you can create the relationship in a single file, the map, instead of having to edit 13 different files.

We've created a simplified relationship table to related cookie topics and recipes in a cookbook (see Figure 6).

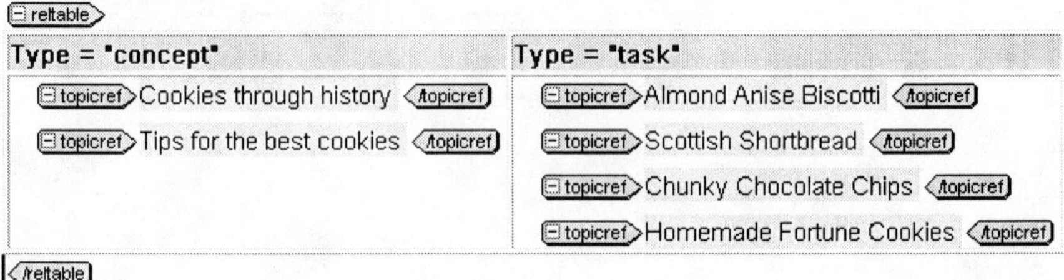

Figure 6: A simple reltable for cookie topics

Usually, a reltable has more rows than this. Each row in the table represents a relationship between topics, which is generally converted to "Related Topics" when the map is processed. Each topic would have related topics as follows:

This Topic	Will have cross references to these topics
Concept: Cookies through history	Concept: Tips for the best cookies Task: Almond Anise Biscotti Task: Scottish Shortbread Task: Chunky Chocolate Chips Task: Homemade Fortune Cookies
Concept: Tips for the best cookies	Concept: Cookies through history Task: Almond Anise Biscotti Task: Scottish Shortbread Task: Chunky Chocolate Chips Task: Homemade Fortune Cookies

<table>
<tr><td>Task: Almond Anise Biscotti</td><td>Concept: Cookies through history
Concept: Tips for the best cookies
Task: Scottish Shortbread
Task: Chunky Chocolate Chips
Task: Homemade Fortune Cookies</td></tr>
<tr><td>Task: Scottish Shortbread</td><td>Concept: Cookies through history
Concept: Tips for the best cookies
Task: Almond Anise Biscotti
Task: Chunky Chocolate Chips
Task: Homemade Fortune Cookies</td></tr>
<tr><td>Task: Chunky Chocolate Chips</td><td>Concept: Cookies through history
Concept: Tips for the best cookies
Task: Almond Anise Biscotti
Task: Scottish Shortbread
Task: Homemade Fortune Cookies</td></tr>
<tr><td>Task: Homemade Fortune Cookies</td><td>Concept: Cookies through history
Concept: Tips for the best cookies
Task: Almond Anise Biscotti
Task: Scottish Shortbread
Task: Chunky Chocolate Chips</td></tr>
</table>

You could build these cross references manually, but you would have to create five cross-references in each of six files. If you added a recipe, you’d have to edit all the files to add the new cross-reference. It’s much easier to just build the relationships in the reltable.

Specialization

There are two perspectives on using an existing XML standard: use it out of the box and live with the benefits and weaknesses, or customize it to eliminate the weaknesses (as much as possible) and make it perfect for you. Both have advantages and disadvantages. (We'll discuss those later.) In DITA, the process and mechanics of customization are called specialization. Specifically, the DITA DTDs have been architected and written to add layers to the base DTDs, to modify elements and attributes, to add new elements and to add new topic types, while still maintaining the ability to easily integrate new versions of the DITA standard as they become available.

Discussions about the merits or needs for specialization can get pretty heated. Some are quite willing to tell you that you don't need to specialize. Others will tell you that you are ignoring the real value of XML and DITA if you don't. We won't describe the mechanics of specialization here. (For more information on the specifics, see Eliot Kimber's excellent tutorial here: http://www.xiruss.org/tutorials/dita-specialization/.) We are, however, going to talk about how to determine whether to specialize DITA for your implementation or to use DITA out of the box.

Why specialize DITA?

Many people say you can use DITA as is, that you don't need to specialize and, in fact, that you shouldn't specialize. But, specialization exists as a key feature of DITA. Why, if it's not needed? The pros vs. con argument can get pretty vigorous at times, but the real answer is "it depends."

Getting to a "yes" or "no" answer, as in "Yes, we need to specialize" or "No, out-of-the box will get us everything we need", will really depend on a clear definition of "need."

So let's refocus for a second. Forget that we'll need to create topics and ditamaps, let's focus on our real job which is to provide good, useful, usable information to our users. That's the end game.

If you're considering moving to DITA, then you probably have issues that are preventing you from achieving good, useful and usable content. Or perhaps you can meet those goals, but you can't do it fast enough. Or you can do it for your English-speaking users, but not for your German-speaking users. Or it costs too much.

To be able to answer the generic vs. specialized question, a clear understanding of what the real problems you’re facing is required which may be one of these:

- content is inconsistent in language
- content is structurally inconsistent (organization or level of detail)
- content is visually inconsistent
- desktop publishing takes too long or is too expensive
- translation takes too long
- translation costs too much

When you’re deciding whether or not to go with XML/DITA and whether or not to specialize, think about the problems that DITA is the solution for or the opportunities to take advantage of. Understanding this is the key.

Vote for production worthiness

IT departments take a lot of grief from business people for their ability to focus on the technical details of potential solutions to the exclusion of all other factors, such as the real business needs that the software is supposed to meet.

But both IT and business stakeholders can be seduced by the lure of fancy functionality. The risk is ending up with a system that does lots of “cool stuff,” but negatively impacts the ability of the people who are suppose to be doing their work with it. The system becomes a distraction or impairment. The system is not “production-worthy.”

A production-worthy system is one that aids the users, rather than one that distracts or impairs them. It provides a range of functionality that aligns nicely with the users’ actual jobs. It’s the system that you want in place when the deadline is fast approaching and the development department is finally signing off their design documents. It’s the system that the users want to use. It’s the system that helps them deliver good, useful and usable content fast.

Two simple questions

When you are making the decision to specialize – assuming that you've already fully decided to go with DITA – carefully consider two questions:

- How do you control the input of content?
- How do you manipulate the content for output?

Remember to make sure that you're providing the right content, in the right format, at the right time, to the right user. Answering the two questions above will help you decide whether or not to specialize.

How do you control the input of content?

You don't need to go to XML or DITA to move to structured authoring. We've helped many clients adopt a structured approach to content while still authoring in tools like Microsoft Word or Adobe FrameMaker. If you develop structured content models and then write the content to fit the models, you are creating structured content. The first problem with this approach is that creating multichannel outputs is more difficult using traditional word-processing or writing packages. The second problem – more important from the authoring perspective – is that tools like Word and Frame (when used in standard, or unstructured, mode) do nothing to help control the structures in the document.

The first thing to do is figure out how well the base topic types fit the content. For example, if you look at the Pumpkin Cheesecake recipe, you can see that it is broken into sections (see Figure 7). We adapted our model to support the sections, but then when we compare the model to the task structure, it doesn't fit directly. The DITA task model does not include structures to break tasks into sections. If you want to use task to capture this kind of recipe, there are two options at this point: create a specialized task that has sections, or capture each section of the recipe in a separate topic.

Recipe 3: Pecan Pumpkin Cheese Cake

Crust

- ¾ cups graham cracker crumbs
- ¼ cup sugar
- ¼ cup melted butter
- ¼ cup light brown sugar
- ½ cup finely chopped pecans

1. Grease a 9 in. spring form pan.
2. Combine ingredients and press into pan up, pushing the crust up about ¼ inch on the side.

Filling

- 1 ½cup solid pumpkin
- 1 ½ tsp cinnamon
- ½ tsp nutmeg
- ½ tsp ginger
- ½ cup light brown sugar
- 2 tbl heavy cream
- 1 tbl cornstarch
- 1 tbl bourbon
- 2 8 oz. packs of cream cheese
- ½ cup sugar
- ½ tsp salt
- 3 eggs
- 1 tsp vanilla

1. Preheat oven to 350
2. In a bowl combine pumpkin, eggs, cinnamon, ginger, nutmeg, salt and brown sugar.
3. In a bowl with an electronic mixer cream together the cream chees and sugar. Beat in cream, cornstarch, vanilla, and bourbon.
4. Combine pumpkin into cream cheese mixture.
5. Pour into crust and bake for 50 to 55 min.
6. Remove from oven and let stand 5 min.

Topping

- 2 cups sour cream
- 2 tbl sugar
- 1 tbl Bourbon

1. Combine all ingredients and spread over top.
2. Bake for 5 mins.
3. Remove and cool then chill thoroughly.
4. Decorate top with pecan halfs.

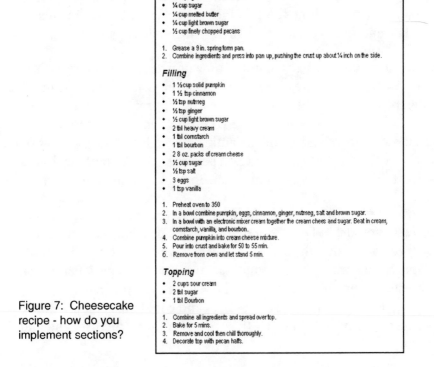

Figure 7: Cheesecake recipe - how do you implement sections?

There are additional questions to ask:

- How many authors contribute?
- Are they located in the same location, in separate buildings, or geographically diverse?
- How experienced are they and are they trained/professional authors?
- How often do they write: as a daily part of their job or sporadically?
- Can you rely on them to remember the structures you want them to follow?
- Can you rely on editing to ensure that structure is consistent?
- Can you rely on peer pressure/professionalism to ensure that structure is consistent?

If you have two authors, sitting next door to each other in the same cubicle farm, who work really, really well together, then probably you could get away with using generic DITA. Two authors means only two ways of doing things and their experience and professionalism could be enough to ensure they maintain consistent structures.

If you have 200 business analysts, some of whom contribute weekly while others contribute a couple of times per year, who reside in different buildings and in some instances different countries, then you might need to specialize your DITA implementation to force specific structures and guide the authors. Two hundred contributors means potentially 200 different perspectives on how content should be written. That's when you need to control the input a bit more.

Following on the recipes example and to decide how to implement the recipe model in DITA, we'd need to decide how to ensure that every recipe follows the same structure. If we have a lot of different people contributing recipes, that's an argument for specializing task to create a recipe topic type. If we have a small staff of authors, working together to create our recipes and cookbooks, then we might be able to get away with using the existing topics structures and and markup.

How do you manipulate the content for output?

DITA topics or XML aren't usually delivered to the end users. Instead, PDFs, or .CHM files, or .HTML files are delivered. You might want to call attention to or distinguish certain content in those outputs to help the user or to make the content most effective.

This is easiest to explain with an example. Let's consider the regular/healthy variations of our recipe. In addition to providing the ability to specify alternate ingredients, we might want to align some of the specific nutritional characteristics in output. For example, we might want to highlight fat content in recipes. We could add a bold tag around the fat value, but it would always be bolded in both regular and healthy versions of the recipe. Alternatively, we could create nutrition tags for our list (see Figure 8) and set a rule in stylesheets that would ensure that fat content would be rendered in bold when a recipe was processed to output a healthy version.

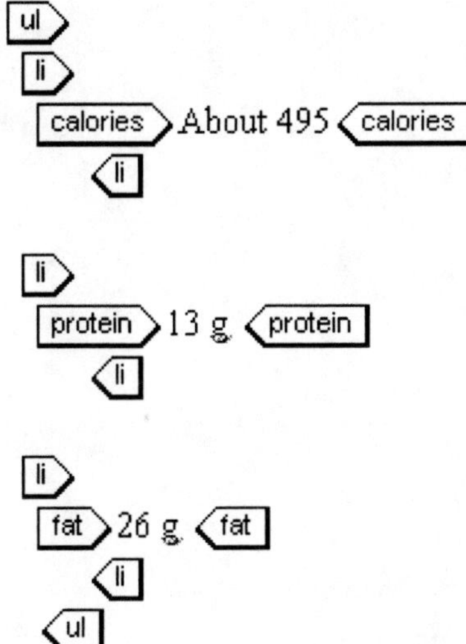

Figure 8: Nutrition elements to help us control formatting

The rule of thumb for rendering specific content is that if you can’t identify it with tags or metadata, you can’t manipulate it in the output format.

So should you specialize DITA?

The decision to specialize DITA or not ultimately boils down to answering these two questions:

- How do you need to control input?
- How will you need to manipulate the output?

And if outof the box DITA won’t let you control or output your content the way you want to, it may make sense to specialize.

Appendix A: DITA topic quick reference

Structural visual reference

```
conbody ,
   (p |
   lq |
   note |
   dl |
   parml |
   ul |
   ol |
   sl |
   pre |
   codeblock |
   msgblock |
   screen |
   lines |
   fig |
   syntaxdiagram |
   imagemap |
   image |
   object |
   table |
   simpletable |
   required-cleanup )*,
   (section |
   example )*
(related-links )?,
```

```
task
   title ,
   titlealts ?,
   ((shortdesc |
   abstract ))?,
   prolog ?,
   taskbody ?,
      prereq ?,
      context ?,
      ((steps |
         (step )+
            cmd ,
            ((info |
            substeps |
               (substep )+
                  cmd ,
                  ((info |
                  tutorialinfo
                  stepxmp ))*
                  stepresult ?
            tutorialinfo |
            stepxmp |
            choicetable |
            choices ))*,
            stepresult ?
      steps-unordered ))?,
      result ?,
      example ?,
      postreq ?
   related-links ?,
```

```
reference
   title ,
   titlealts ?,
   ((shortdesc |
   abstract ))?,
   prolog ?,
   refbody ?,
      (section |
      refsyn |
      example |
      table |
      simpletable |
      properties |
      data |
      data-about |
      foreign |
      unknown )*
   related-links ?,
   reference *
```

Figure 1: A visual illustration of the structure of topics. The bold indicates that it is a container (contains other elements). The indents visually show the contents of each container.

Concept

concept	Concept topics answer the question "what is?" They provide background information that users must know before they can successfully work with a product or interface. Its structure is only slightly more semantic than topic.
title	The <title> element contains a heading for the topic.

titlealts
    searchtitle
    navtitle
	<titlealts> is a container for alternate versions of the title for search results or for navigation windows.
	
	<searchtitle> is used to create a title element at the top of the resulting XHTML file.
	
	<navtitle> may be used to create navigation panels when the DITA topics are part of an HTML-based Help or information system.
	
	Typically, these are used with long main topic titles that might be too long for a navigation widget or too long for the browser bar.

shortdesc Or abstract shortdesc	The short description is the initial paragraph-like content of a topic, or it can be embedded in an abstract element. The short description should be a single, concise paragraph containing one or two sentences of no more than 50 words. It is also intended to be used as a link preview and for searching. You cannot have multiple paragraphs in a shortdesc. Use the <shortdesc> element when the first paragraph of topic content is simple enough to be suitable for use as a link preview or for summaries. Otherwise use the <abstract> element instead to provide richer content around the <shortdesc>. Abstract is para.class plus <shortdesc>.
prolog	The <prolog> element contains the metadata elements of the topic. Much of the metadata inside the <prolog> will not be displayed with the topic on output, but may be used by processes that generate search indexes or customize navigation.

conbody	The <conbody> element is the main body-level element inside a concept topic. It is a container for some combination of <section>, <example> and para.class elements
section example	Sections are used to organize subsets of information that are directly related to the topic and are used the way that headings are used in any other sort of content/ document. Note that DITA currently only allows one level of section. The <example> element is a section with the specific role of containing examples that illustrate or support the current topic. The <example> element has the same content model as <section>, which is <title> followed by <para.class>
related-links	The related information links of a topic (<related-links> element) are stored in a special section following the body of the topic. After a topic is processed into its final output form, the related links are usually displayed at the end of the topic, although some Web-based Help systems might display them in a separate navigation frame.

Task

task	Tasks are the main building blocks for task-oriented user assistance. They generally provide step-by-step instructions that will enable a user to perform a task.
title	The <title> element contains a heading for the topic.
titlealts searchtitle navtitle	<titlealts> is a container for alternate versions of the title for search results or for navigation windows. <searchtitle> is used to create a title element at the top of the resulting XHTML file. <navtitle> may be used to create navigation panels when the DITA topics are part of an HTML-based Help or information system. Typically, these are used with long main topic titles that might be too long for a navigation widget or too long for the browser bar.
shortdesc Or abstract shortdesc	The short description is the initial paragraph-like content of a topic, or it can be embedded in an abstract element. The short description should be a single, concise paragraph containing one or two sentences of no more than 50 words. It is also intended to be used as a link preview and for searching. You cannot have multiple paragraphs in a shortdesc. Use the <shortdesc> element when the first paragraph of topic content is simple enough to be suitable for use as a link preview or for summaries. Otherwise use the <abstract> element instead to provide richer content around the <shortdesc>. Abstract is para.class plus <shortdesc>.
prolog	The <prolog> element contains the metadata elements of the topic. Much of the metadata inside the <prolog> will not be displayed with the topic on output, but may be used by processes that generate search indexes or customize navigation.

taskbody	The <taskbody> element is the main body-level element inside a task topic. It is a container with the following elements in this order: <prereq>, <context>, <steps>, <result>, <example> and <postreq>. Each of the body sections are optional.
prereq	The pre-requisite (<prereq>) section of a task should document things the user needs to know or do before starting the current task. Prerequisite links will be placed in a list after the related-links section; on output the <prereq> links from the related-links section are added to the <prereq> section.
context	The <context> section of a task provides background information for the task. This information helps the user understand what the purpose of the task is and what they will gain by completing the task. This section should be brief and does not replace or recreate a concept topic on the same subject, although the context section may include some conceptual information.
steps	The <steps> section of a task provides the main content of the task topic. The task is described as a series of steps that the user must follow to accomplish the task. One or more <steps> elements is required inside the <steps> section. Two or more steps appear as an ordered list. A single step appears as a paragraph. If all of the contained steps are simple (that is, have no more than a <cmd> element each) then the step list should default to compact. Otherwise it should be formatted as uncompact (with blank lines between each step on output).
step	The <step> element represents an action that a user must follow to accomplish a task. Each step in a task must contain a command <cmd> element which describes the particular action the user must do to accomplish the overall task. The step element can also contain information <info>, substeps <substeps>, tutorial information <tutorialinfo>, a step example <stepxmp>, choices <choices> or a stepresult <stepresult>, although these are optional.

cmd	The command (<cmd>) element is required as the first element inside a <step>. It provides the active voice instruction to the user for completing the step and should not be more than one sentence. If the step needs additional explanation, this can follow the <cmd> element inside an <info > element. The substructure of <cmd> is text and phrase.class elements.
info	The information element (<info>) occurs inside a <step> element to provide additional information about the step.
substeps	The <substeps> element allows a step to be broken down into a series of separate actions and should be used only if necessary. Try to describe the steps of a task in a single level of steps. If more than one level of substep nesting is required, you should probably rewrite the task to simplify it. A <substep> element has the same structure as a <step>, except it does not allow lists of choices or substeps within it in order to prevent unlimited nesting of steps.
tutorialinfo	The tutorial info (<tutorialinfo>) element contains additional information that is useful when the task is part of a tutorial.
stepxmp	The step example (<stepxmp>) element is used to illustrate a step of a task. The example can be a couple of words or an entire paragraph.
choicetable	The <choicetable> element contains a series of optional choices available within a step of a task. A choice table could look something like this: Option | Description A | This is the description of the option A. ... | ... ... | ... ... | ... ... | ... ... | ...

choices	The <choices> element contains a list of <choice> elements. It is used when the user will need to choose one of several actions while performing the steps of a task. <choice> elements are formatted as bullets.
stepresult	The <stepresult> element provides information on the expected outcome of a step. If a user interface is being documented, the outcome could describe a dialog box opening, or the appearance of a progress indicator. Step results are useful to assure a user that they are on track, but should not be used for every step, as this quickly becomes tedious. The substructure of <stepresult> is para.class.
steps-unordered	Like the <steps> element, the <steps-unordered> section of a task provides the main content of the task topic, but particularly for cases in which the order of steps may vary from one situation to another. One or more steps are required inside the <steps-unordered> section. Two or more steps appear as an unordered list. A single step appears as a paragraph
result	The <result> element describes the expected outcome for the task as a whole. The substructure of <postreq> is para.class.
example	The <example> element is a section with the specific role of containing examples that illustrate or support the current topic. The <example> element has the same content model as <section>, which is <title> followed by <para.class> DITA uses <example> to contain both discussion and sample code or outputs. Hence, in a DITA topic, to represent programming code and results within the discussion in an example, use the <codeblock> and <systemoutput> elements within the example element. For lines of text, use the <lines> element. For pre-formatted text such as email headers, use the <pre> element.

postreq	The <postreq> element describes steps or tasks that the user should do after the successful completion of the current task. It is often supported by links to the next task or tasks in the <related-links> section. The substructure of <postreq> is para.class.
related-links	The related information links of a topic (<related-links> element) are stored in a special section following the body of the topic. After a topic is processed into its final output form, the related links are usually displayed at the end of the topic, although some Web-based Help systems might display them in a separate navigation frame.

Reference

reference	Reference topics are the database topics of DITA. That is, they are used to provide the quick lookup sorts of stuff found in various types of documentation. If something is best documented in a lookup table, it is probably a reference topic. The reference topic was originally designed for documenting software products, which is evident from the defined sub structures.
title	The <title> element contains a heading for the topic.
titlealts searchtitle navtitle	<titlealts> is a container for alternate versions of the title for search results or for navigation windows. <searchtitle> is used to create a title element at the top of the resulting XHTML file. <navtitle> may be used to create navigation panels when your DITA topics are part of an HTML-based Help or information system. Typically, these are used when you have long main topic titles that might be too long for a navigation widget or too long for the browser bar.
shortdesc Or abstract shortdesc	The short description is the initial paragraph-like content of a topic, or it can be embedded in an abstract element. The short description should be a single, concise paragraph containing one or two sentences of no more than 50 words. It is also intended to be used as a link preview and for searching. You cannot have multiple paragraphs in a shortdesc. Use the <shortdesc> element when the first paragraph of the topic content is simple enough to be suitable for use as a link preview or for summaries. Otherwise use the <abstract> element instead to provide richer content around the <shortdesc>. Abstract is para.class plus <shortdesc>.

prolog	The <prolog> element contains the metadata elements of the topic. Much of the metadata inside the <prolog> will not be displayed with the topic on output, but may be used by processes that generate search indexes or customize navigation.
refbody	The <refbody> element is the main body-level element inside a reference topic. It is a container for some combination of <section>, <example>, <refsyn>, <properties>, and para.class elements.
refsyn	<refsyn> is a special section for syntax information in reference topics. The structure is the same as <section>, but the semantic name identifies it as specifically for reference content.
properties	The <properties> element provides structures for listing properties for the current topic. **Property Type** | **Property Value** | **Property Description** *Property Type* | *Property Value* | *Property Description*
related-links	The related information links of a topic (<related-links> element) are stored in a special section following the body of the topic. After a topic is processed into its final output form, the related links are usually displayed at the end of the topic, although some Web-based Help systems might display them in a separate navigation frame.

Appendix B - Prolog Metadata

The software-centric history of the prolog metadata can be seen in related elements such as *platform*, *prognum* and *component*. However, they can be implemented in a wide variety of ways that are not related to software development. In addition, if elements are not required, they don't have to be used.

Term Name	Description
Prolog	The prolog element is similar to the html element <head> that lives at the top of all Web pages. Generally, the information contained in it is not seen or displayed; rather it's used by the system to manage the content. This is the "top level" element for all the others shown below.
Author	The person or organization who created the content.
Copyright	This container holds the copyright information, comprising the *copyrholder* and the *copyryear*. You can have more than one copyright holder, so you can have more than one entry.
Copyrholder	This contains the name of he copyright holder. It may be an individual or organization as defined by local copyright laws.
Copyryear	This contains the year of copyright.
Critdates	Container holding the critical dates in the lifecycle of the information. Typically includes creation and revision dates.
Created	Contains the date the content was created.
Revised	This is used to track various change dates in the life of the information.
Metadata	Contains audience and product information. This element contains the metadata elements *audience*, *category*, *keywords*, *prodinfo* and *othermeta*.
Audience	Audience defines the intended audience for the topic. This includes the type, job and the experience level of the reader. For example, you could define the audience for a topic to be a programmer, who would be programming (rather than managing or administering) with an expert experience level. Because a particular Topic may have more than one audience, you can have more than one audience defined in the metadata.

Category	You can identify categories to help you identify or find information. These categories are specific to your needs and can be fully customized. For example, you might have a category for large products, another for small ones. Categories might be based on color, usage, price or any other identifiable characteristic that is useful to you and your users.
Keywords	Contains a list of keywords that will be used to find the information. You can have multiple keywords. Note that if the information is output to HTML, these keywords will be copied into the <header> section as page level keywords.
Prodinfo	This is used to provide specific information about the product that is the subject of the current topic.
Brand	The brand name of the product (Black and Decker, for example).
Prodname	The name of the product (distinct from the brand name – so Drill, rather than Black and Decker).
Prognum	This is focused on software development, but could be used for any product tracking number.
Vrmlist	This container element holds the list of vrm elements describing the version, revision and modifications for the product.
Vrm	These are the individual Version, Revision and Modification notes for the product topic. It's expected that there will be more than one entry, as the first would be for the release of the product, with subsequent entries for various revisions and modifications.
Series	If there are multiple series of products, this would be captured here.
Platform	This is focused on software development (and was specifically intended to identify the operating system and/or hardware required to support a particular program).
Featnum	Contains the feature number of the referenced product or information.

Component	This is designed for products that are comprised of smaller independent components. It is ideally suited for software products (where different components can be installed separately to make a finished product – main program, import/export filters, Help files, training, etc.) but can also be used for any inter-related information.
Othermeta	This is the “messy kitchen stuff” drawer of the DITA world. Specifically designed to manage information that’s not captured by the existing metadata, you can create and define this element to contain anything you need. When exported as HTML, the information in this element is exported as HTML metadata.
Permissions	This defines the level of access granted to specific users. The applicability of this element depends on the specific filtering and formatting capabilities of your system.
Publisher	The person or organization who distributes the content.
Resourceid	This is a unique identifier for each piece of content. It was specifically designed to allow applications to receive information in a particular format.
Source	The source points to the resource (a document, URL, description, etc.) that was the source (in whole or in part) for the existing topic.

Appendix C: A history of DITA

A good way to start learning about and understanding DITA (Darwin Information Typing Architecture) is at the beginning.

The origins

In the beginning, all the way back to the 1970's, there were disparate software applications that really did not play well together at all. Charles Goldfarb, a researcher at IBM, observed that many systems at IBM could not share information with each other, that they each used their own "language" (incompatible file formats) to format the text. SGML (Standard Generalized Markup Language) was born out of a project to build a system for creating, managing and publishing legal documents. A markup language is a set of annotations (tags) on text that describe how the text is to be structured, laid out, or formatted. HTML is the most widely known markup language. Any application that formats text has an underlying markup language. For example, RTF (Rich Text Format) is the underlying markup language for Microsoft Word.

SGML was based on the following three principles:

- Computers need to be able to share files in a common format. (they need to "speak" the same language).
- The mark up of a document has to be extensible.
- There needs to be a way to identify the structure of documents so that different documents of the same type will share the same structure or rules.

As the Internet came into being and developed, the community recognized that HTML had its limitations (insufficient tag set, could only describe format and not the content itself) and that SGML was essentially overkill. So a working group under the World Wide Web Consortium (W3C) began work on XML.

The goals of the W3C in developing XML include the following:

- Web-based delivery
- open standard

- based on SGML
- formal and concise
- easy to author and create
- easy to develop applications for
- extensible

The first point is extremely important. To be suitable for the Web, the working group needed to create a streamlined version of SGML—SGML Lite—that would provide a lightweight markup standard, with all of the needed features and without the bulkiness that would overwhelm the Web. XML was that streamlined version of SGML.

XML has been a great success. Use has spread beyond content markup to all sorts of other business and software applications.

Why XML in content creation?

From a content and publishing perspective, XML has become an extremely important technology for both big and small publishers. For complex content management with information reuse, XML is the technology of choice.

XML provides the ability to do a whole lot more than what can be done with traditional tools. The characteristics of XML that best support publishing are:

- structured content
- separation of content and format
- XSL (eXtensible Stylesheet Language) stylesheets

XML and structured content

Authors typically have a high-level understanding of the concept of structured content. For example, they understand that books have front matter, body chapters, and back matter. Authors may also recognize repeatable structures at a lower level. Chapters have titles, overviews, sections containing the "meat" of the chapter, and a summary. Some authors can even describe the structure in individual sections, for example, a procedure.

However, when you examine similar information products, you find that structures are not consistent from product to product. Even among documents of the same type, structures will vary from author to author, from department to department, from division to division. Even information written by a single author will vary over time. This is a problem for a number of reasons.

First, for users, the impact of changes in structure can range from distracting to confusing. People, as creatures of habit, get used to seeing things in the same places. When things move, it takes us time to get used to the changes. Changes in structure may be seen as inconsistencies, and may lead the user to distrust the material.

Inconsistency also has a major impact on reuse. Effective reuse is built on predictability. The initial analysis of the content and user's needs for that content will define the structure of your information products, like manuals or Help systems, as well as specific types of content, like concepts or procedures. If authors cannot comfortably predict the structure and detail of the content in the Content Management System (CMS), they will be reluctant to reuse it, and will be more likely to recreate it.

With all that, why do we need DITA?

First of all, starting an XML implementation from scratch can be expensive. The process of creating content models, Document Type Definition (DTDs) or schemas, and stylesheets can be quite time-consuming. Being able to start from an existing markup standard like DITA takes you a giant step along the development timeline.

DITA was developed primarily by IBM in a response to the changing needs of their business. Those needs are the same needs that we all face:

- figuring out how to get products to market faster
- finding ways to reduce unnecessary expenses
- delivering content in an increasing number of output formats
- finding ways to react faster to changing demands (more flexibility)

- increasing the effectiveness of content

Changes in corporate goals, changes in technology, changes in customer expectations and needs all have to be met. DITA is the mechanism IBM chose to meet those needs.

Recognizing that DITA would benefit writing departments everywhere, IBM has passed the standard to the Organization for the Advancement of Structured Information Standards (OASIS) a not-for-profit, international consortium that drives the development, convergence, and adoption of e-business standards. As an OASIS standard, DITA is at version 1.1, with 1.2 in development.

Design goals

Before discussing the details of DITA, it's useful to understand some of the goals that led to the development of the standard.

Move away from focus on books to multiple formats and outputs

One of the largest impacts of technology on information development is the addition of so many new formats for delivering information. No one just delivers a user guide (book) any more. There is an increasing need for information to be delivered in multiple formats. While some improvements have been made, many of the book-based technologies in use today are not efficient tools for creating multiple outputs from a single source of content. Format conversions have been simplified, but working in a book-based paradigm has made it difficult to support other information types that do not need the same kinds of book structures. The standards that have been available to date, like DocBook, have been book-based.

Move away from SGML to XML

IBM had been using SGML for some time but recognized that XML, with its stated focus on Internet applicability, was a better option. Web-based formats and delivery have become crucial tools for delivering effective information to users.

Move towards the trend to minimalism

The goal of information development and delivery should be "the right information, at the right time, in the right format, to the right person." For IBM, that meant reducing information "glut," lessening the volume of irrelevant information presented to users, and focusing on providing only the information that users *need*. This approach reduces both the time it takes to create and maintain information, facilitates quicker information delivery, and reduces the effort required to keep information up-to-date.

Provide more flexibility in structures and move away from "monolithic" DTDs

The trend in the past was to create a Document Type Definition (DTD) focused on the needs of single departments and specific information products they produce. This approach, however, can have a negative impact on wide-scale reuse, as content created by one department may be difficult to reuse in other departments. DITA is intended to provide a mechanism that establishes a clear base of common structures, making it easier to create specific structures needed by different departments.

Support maximum reuse

Reuse is today's best practice for information developers. DITA was developed specifically to promote content reuse and reduce redundant information.

Benefits of DITA

Considering the benefits that come with SGML and XML, you might wonder why you should consider DITA instead of just developing your own SGML or XML markup scheme. That might be the right way to go; there are still many, many applications which cry out for SGML or XML solutions other than DITA. And there are many other XML solutions that compete with DITA, like DocBook and S1000D. So what are the arguments in favor of DITA?

First, **starting from scratch is expensive**. DITA is an open standard that includes a set of predefined structures for capturing topic-based content and gives you a set of tags and structures to use as-is or as a starting point for creating your own specialized structures.

DITA is **output independent**. That is, as a basic principle of its use, topics are written in DITA to be output into other formats as necessary. When authoring in Microsoft Word or standard FrameMaker, for example, you are authoring in an interface that has been designed and optimized for creating paper output.

DITA was **designed to support reuse**. From the beginning, DITA's developers recognized reuse as a best-principle of content creation. By focusing on the information, rather than the output, you can write information once and use it in other formats and contexts as needed. This does take planning to get the structures right, effort to teach people to write in a new way, and discipline to actually write that way. But you can save money, save time, and improve quality if you do it right.

Alternatives to DITA

DITA is not the first XML initiative to become popular or widely used. Companies implementing XML solutions have always had alternatives, including building custom DTDs from scratch. Industry-standard DTDs, like DocBook, and S1000D have also existed for people to use. Each have strengths and weaknesses as does any initiative or approach.

DocBook

If you approached XML editor or content management system vendors five years ago, they would at some point during the conversation ask you if you had considered DocBook. For publishing, it was really the first "industry-standard" DTD for the publications focus.

It was originally developed as an SGML markup language for converting, sharing, and ultimately authoring technical manuals for UNIX computer systems. Eventually, its development was taken over by a Technical Committee (TC) of the Organization for the Advancement of Structured Information Standards (OASIS).

The standard has undergone multiple revisions since its initial version, with wide contributions from many users. As a result, it's a very robust model, which accommodates pretty much any model of documentation guide imaginable. However, with over 300 individual elements, it's very complex and can be difficult to use. To help aleviate the problem, the DocBook developers have designed the model and Document Type Definition (DTD) to facilitate the use of a customization layer. This layer is built on top of DocBook to simplify the models actually used by authors.

DocBook is a stable, tested, mature software documentation model. It's been used and refined over a long period of time and over varied applications. As a result, it has built-in models to cover most, if not all, typical software documentation applications. DocBook is not just for technical documentation, though many organizations such as publishers and companies that write a lot of articles and reports use DocBook.

However, DocBook has lost some of its appeal in the last few years for several reasons. DocBook:

- was designed for the creation of "books" not Web materials
- does not support reuse well
- is overly complex

DocBook is still in use and is not likely to go away for a long time to come. DocBook is appropriate for content that is largely print-based. DocBook is frequently used for narrative documents and in areas like Government.

DocBook is seeing a resurgence in the increased use of XQuery. XQuery is a recommendation of the World Wide Web Consortium (W3C) and is supported by all the major database engines (IBM, Oracle, Microsoft, etc.). XQuery is to XML what SQL is to database tables. That is, it's a language for extracting data from XML repositories, just as SQL is a query language for extracting data from relational databases. In fact, XQuery is semantically similar to SQL, but is designed specifically for finding and extracting elements and attributes from XML documents. Many companies are converting their existing content to DocBook since XQuery can:

- query/search any XML-based content, regardless of schema
- automatically extract and reassemble content in any desired configuration

- repurpose content without pre-chunking.

S1000D

S1000D is an international standard for the procurement and production of technical publications. Initially developed by AECMA (Association Europeene des Constructeurs de Materiel Aerospatial) to manage maintenance materials for military aircraft, its maintenance has been assumed by AeroSpace and Defence Industries of Europe (ASD) and the Aerospace Industries Association of America (AIA). It's controlled by the Technical Publications Specification Management Group (TPSMG). This ensures that no one player can unduly influence the creation or management of the standard, and that all viewpoints and requirements are judged in a fair manner.

Although it was initially designed to manage content for maintenance information, its use rapidly expanded to include crew related technical documents. Later expansion of the specification incorporated non-aviation (often described in the literature as land and sea platforms) military equipment technical documents.

The key feature of S1000D is the ability to store content in reusable and stand-alone "data modules". A data module is defined as "the smallest self contained information unit" in a document or publication. In order to be defined as a data module, the information must be understandable when viewed with only graphical support.

Because these modules are stand-alone and stored in a common source database (CSDB), information can be created once, and reused many times in many locations.

Other benefits of using the S1000D specification for managing information include it:

- is an internationally recognized standard, applicable across a broad industry
- is non-proprietary, so you are not locked into a single developer or application
- is designed to handle the issues of "legacy data"

- reduces cost due to reuse
- increases accuracy due to verifiable content

Unlike DITA, which is designed to be customizable (or "specialized" to use DITA terminology), S1000D is designed to be implemented in a more regimented manner. Although this does make implementation more challenging, it ensures that the integrity of the data types and related content is more easily maintained between organizations and applications.

What is XML?

XML is a set of rules for defining markup languages. We're all familiar with markup languages, with HTML being the most common example available. We've all looked at HTML code and in many cases we create content directly in HTML.

The XML standard (currently at version 1.1) is based on the SGML standard, which was designed with many of the same goals as XML. XML has been streamlined—reduced in complexity and capability—from SGML to make it practical for the Internet. However, XML retains enough of the characteristics to make it very effective for all sorts of publishing and specifically content management for publishing.

The advantage that the XML standard brings is that it allows you to define a tagset that meets the specific needs of your content. It's a set of rules for creating markup languages (like HTML). Unlike HTML where the tags are defined, XML allows you to create the tags to suit the needs of your content and your authors.

But what *IS* XML?

XML can best be described by walking through a sample of XML markup.

XML files are made up primarily of elements and attributes. Elements have start tags, end tags, and content. Attributes have names and values.

```
<Procedure Audience="All">
<Title>Logging On to AccSoft </Title>
<Text>You must log on to the system before you can complete
any tasks.
</Text>
<Intro>To log on to AccSoft:</Intro>
<ProcedureSteps>
<Step>Double-click the AccSoft application</Step>
<Step>Type your USERID into the <Fieldname>Name</Fieldname>
field</ Step>
<Step>Type your password into the <Fieldname>Password</
Fieldname> field.</Step>
<Step>Click the OK button to log on to AccSoft.</Step>
</ProcedureSteps>
</Procedure>
```

In the sample, <Title> is a start tag. Tags are enclosed by angle brackets. </ Title> is an end tag: end tags always begin with a slash (/) after the opening angle bracket. The "Title" element is the start tag (<Title>), the end tag(</ Title>), and everything in between. "audience" is an attribute name; "advanced" is the value. The combination of name and value comprise the attribute.

In the example, some elements, like Title, Text, and Intro, just contain data. Others, like Procedure, and ProcedureSteps, contain other elements. Some Step elements contain both data and elements (Fieldname).

What do XML Tags Do?

XML tags:

- describe your document's content (meaningful tag and attribute names)
- describe the structure of your document (document/node tree)
- indicate hierarchy of data through embedded elements
- do not include formatting or "style" characteristics

Comparing XML and HTML

There are a number of differences between HTML and XML. HTML is a set of tags that you can use to present content in a browser. Its primary application is presentation. It was not designed to capture structure. On the other hand, XML allows you to create your own markup languages with a focus on capturing the structure of content. The XML standard does not provide any specific capability for presentation.

From w3schools (http://www.w3schools.com/xml/xml_whatis.asp):

- XML was designed to describe data and to focus on what data is.
- HTML was designed to display data and to focus on how data looks.

A procedure in HTML

Consider what the sample procedure above might look like if it was marked up with HTML.

```
<h2>Logging On to AccSoft </h2>
<p>You must log on to the system before you can complete any
tasks.</p>
<h3>To log on to AccSoft:</h3>
<ol>
<li>Double-click the AccSoft application</li>
<li>Type your USERID into the <i>Name field</i></li>
<li>Type your password into the <i>Password</i> field.</li>
<li>Click the OK button to log on to AccSoft.</li>
</ol>
```

The h2 tag indicates that you have a second-level heading, but you must interpret the content to determine that the content is a procedure.

Advantages of XML?

The advantages of XML are that it:

- promotes consistency through structured documents. Documents follow the same structures, with similar documents having the same content pieces.
- separates structure from format allowing authors to focus on writing.
- enables single-sourcing (component reuse). Structured information is easy to break into individual components for reuse or repurposing.
- enables multiple output (formats and content). Publishing information is isolated from the content and is easily changed/replaced/added to.
- enables dynamic documents. Documents can be built from components, enabling you to select components dynamically.
- increases output flexibility. Structured information is easy to manipulate to reconfigure or republish.

An example

Consider a procedure. The content model for a procedure could be expressed as:

- a procedure contains a title
- followed by a description of the procedure
- followed by a heading to introduce actual steps
- followed by one or more steps
- followed by links to related procedures

The content model is a specific relationship of elements of content.

DTDs and schemas

In XML, structure can be defined in a schema or DTD. They specifically define all of the elements (tags) that can be used in a document. It also defines the relationship of those elements to other elements. You can specify the hierarchy of elements ("a chapter contains..."), the order of elements, even the number of elements.

DTDs and schemas:

- are formal documents, written in a particular syntax, which specifies an XML vocabulary (set of tags)
- describe which elements and entities may appear in associated documents, including:
  - elements
  - attributes
  - child elements
  - number of children
  - sequences of elements
  - mixed content
  - empty elements
  - text declarations
- formally documents content models

Advantages of schemas over DTDs?

DTDs and schemas are similar in that they both define the required structure of a document. However, schemas are, in effect, an updated version of DTDs. As XML use on the Web increased, developers realized that DTDs were limited in what they could do, and that a more able mechanism for defining structure was needed. Schemas provide that increase in capability.

Schemas include all of the capabilities of DTDs, plus:

- they are written as well-formed XML documents (DTDs are created using a different language)
- data can be validated based on built-in and user-defined data types
- programmers can more easily create complex and reusable content models
- schemas support local and global variables in the XML document

The two key differences (for authoring and publication) between schemas and DTDs are that schemas are written using a specific XML markup language, while DTDs require you to learn a separate, unique language and, most importantly, schemas offer what developers like to call "rich datatyping capabilities for elements and attributes". That translates to enabling much greater control over the structure of content and the content itself. For example, in a DTD, you can create a "year" element as part of a date. You can also specify that the "year" element contains only content and not other elements. But that is all you can specify within the element. A DTD can only specify the correct arrangements of elements to other elements. In a schema, not only can you define a "year" element, you can also specify that it must be 4 characters long and that all characters must be numeric (1, 2, 3, ...) It allows control over the data itself.

A schema can be invaluable for authoring and publication. Many authors take as much time figuring out the structure they need to write to as they do actually crafting the information. Do I need an overview? Should my procedure have an introduction? With a schema, you can mandate the structure that is required. This consistency is also very valuable for the users of the information. Consistency leads to predictability. Users learn where information is to be found and can automatically navigate to it, finding what they need quickly and efficiently.

For structural consistency, having a defined structure in a schema is important. However, you need to be able to confirm that your content matches the content model defined in the schema. This functionality is provided by specialized tools called parsers that can read a schema and enforce the structural rules defined in it. The parser "reads" the document and reports an error when the structure and content do not match the schema.

Most XML authoring tools have parsers built in, to parse the content as you enter it, and ensure that the elements and content match the requirements of the schema. Some authoring tools will only allow you to enter elements in their defined places and will not allow you to enter elements that "break the rules" of the schema. By providing authors with an editor and a schema you can ensure that all of your information products are structurally consistent.

Separation of content and format

Word processing and desktop publishing tools revolutionized the way technical documentation was created. Authors quickly gained the opportunity to take formatting control over their documents. The long lead times and production cycles of formal layout for printing were eliminated as authors began producing their own camera-ready, hot-off-the-laser printer copy.

However, these new formatting capabilities come with issues. For some, having responsibility is a burden, for others, a distraction. Many authors become more concerned with how content looks, rather that what the content says.

XML by itself is not acceptable for display to the average user. It must be formatted for presentation.

There are a number of technologies available for formatting. XML presentation is XSL (eXtensible Style Language). Unlike traditional stylesheets, which provide only formatting commands, XSL is a powerful mechanism for both transforming and formatting XML documents.

Using a stylesheet gives you the ability to describe all of your formatting needs, including fonts, colors, sizes, margins, bullets, list numbers, and so on, in a WYSIWYG editor.

XSL

Of course, your job is probably not to deliver XML files, but rather PDF, or HTML, or Help files in some format. For content management and publishing, a large measure of the advantages of XML comes from XSL, the eXtensible stylesheet Language. You use XSL to transform (or convert or publish) to the output formats you want to deliver.

XSL:

- is XML markup language itself (there is an XSL vocabulary)
- can format content for online display or for paper-based delivery

- can add constant text or graphics (like the icons in our warning example)
- can filter content
- can sort or reorder content
- is really divided into three parts:
    - XSLT - a transformation language
    - XSL-FO (XSL Formatting Objects) - a language used to format XML
    - XPath

But rather than simply formatting the information in a document, XSL gives you the ability to transform it into something else. That is, you can manipulate the information to reorder, repeat, filter out information, or even add information based on details in the file. This is where XSL transformations, also known as XSLT, fits in. XSLT allows you to transform an XML document into another markup language. The most common use of XSLT is to transform information to HTML for display on the Web. But XSLT can also be used to convert information from XML into markup for wireless display, for transmission to PDAs and Web-enabled cell phones.

The flexibility of XSL and its pieces is extremely valuable for information publication and presentation. Unlike traditional tools, which associate one stylesheet with one document, you can create any number of stylesheets for a single XML document or information type. If you want to post the document on the Web, create an XSL stylesheet to HTML. For wireless, create an XSL stylesheet to WML.

Despite the unstoppable growth of the Internet and display technologies, paper will continue to be a required output for information. XSL-FO has been designed for that purpose. If you want paper, create an XSL-FO stylesheet. XSL-FO (XSL Formatting Objects) provides stylesheet capabilities for converting XML to paper-based formats like PDF. It provides for all of the required formatting, including page layouts, headers, footers, recto/verso (odd/even) pages, portrait and landscape pages, and so on.

When the information is ready to publish, you can process the file against all stylesheets simultaneously and get all required outputs at the same time.

Index

O

P

R

S

T

W

X

The Rockley Group

The Rockley Group helps content managers and authors meet the increasing demands of creating, distributing and managing the content they create. Our team of experienced analysts brings a wide variety of expertise to the table and can help you avoid expensive pitfalls. Organizations of all sizes — from small, privately-owned firms to multi-national Fortune 500 companies — trust us with their most important content projects. We serve clients in the Financial, Life Sciences and High Technology industries, as well as others in the Communication, Marketing and Retail Sales markets. We've developed content reuse solutions that reduce the cost and effort to produce complex information products including: marketing collateral, software documentation, online help, customer support materials, human resources content, as well as regulatory documents for pharmaceutical and medical device manufacturers.

The Rockley Group was established in 1995 to serve the information community. Our team has experience in customer-centric content management, design and creation of sales and marketing materials, technical support strategies, online documentation, web design, instructional design and content reuse (single sourcing). Our team of experienced analysts, information architects, project managers, information technologists and technology partners provides our clients with the skills necessary to deliver content management solutions that work.

Ann Rockley

Ann Rockley is President of The Rockley Group, Inc. She has an international reputation for developing intelligent content management strategies and underlying information architecture. Rockley is a frequent contributor to trade and industry publications and a keynote speaker at numerous conferences in North America and Europe. Ann Rockley has been referred to as a "luminary" in the content management industry.

She has been instrumental in establishing the field in online documentation, single sourcing (content reuse), unified content strategies and content management best practices. Rockley led

Content Management Professionals, a member organization that fosters the sharing of content management information, practices and strategies to a prestigious eContent 100 award in 2005. Ann co-chairs the OASIS DITA for Enterprise Business Documents subcommittee.

Rockley is a Fellow of the Society for Technical Communication and has a Master of Information Science from the University of Toronto. Rockley is the author of the best-selling book "Managing Enterprise Content: A Unified Content Strategy", New Riders Publishing ISBN 0-7357-1306-5.

Steve Manning

Steve Manning is a Principal with The Rockley Group with over 10 years' of experience in content management.

Steve has helped many clients make decisions about content management, including developing new content management visions, deciding on the need for XML; identifying and selecting technologies for authoring, content management, and production; revising processes for new content management visions. Steve has also participated in the implementation of content management technology, creating custom DTDs, revising existing DTDs (including DITA specializations), creating and revising stylesheets and writing implementation plans for integration vendors.

Steve teaches "Enterprise Content Management" at the University of Toronto and is a frequent speaker at conferences (ASIS, AUGI, STC, ACM SIGDOC, DIA, etc.) on the subject of XML and Content Management. Steve is a co-author of Managing Enterprise Content: A Unified Content Strategy with Ann Rockley. He is an active participant on the OASIS DITA Technical Committee and Enterprise Business Documents subcommittee.

Charles Cooper

Charles Cooper is Vice President of The Rockley Group, Inc.

Cooper has over 10 years' experience in user experience, taxonomy and workflow design. He teaches, facilitates modeling sessions and develops taxonomy and workflow strategies.

He has facilitated sessions in these areas, evaluated existing materials and created new ones. He has assisted companies by analyzing their current workflow and taxonomy systems, helped create new ones and worked to ensure that they were maintained on a consistent basis. He has analyzed content lifecycles for engineering and user information and has organized new methods and processes for publishing and information dissemination. He has assisted companies by analyzing their current web sites (internal and external), to identify areas of improvement, design the user interface, design and conduct usability tests, develop a taxonomy and metadata and design effective workflow.

He has a strong background in process and business planning and believes that taxonomies, structure, organization and workflow must be designed to support the company as they work to provide products and services that their customers need.

Breinigsville, PA USA
18 July 2010

241920BV00005BB/4/P